Training Your Pit Bull

Joe Stahlkuppe

Illustrations by Michele Earle-Bridges

BARRON'S

About the Author

Joe Stahlkuppe is a widely read magazine and newspaper pet columnist, author, pet radio host, and freelance feature writer. An acknowledged pet expert, he has written over a dozen books for Barron's. An ordained pastor, Joe is a lifetime member of the Disabled American Veterans (DAV) and Vietnam Veterans of America, where he serves as a volunteer chaplain. He lives on a small farm near Birmingham, Alabama with his wife of thirty years, Cathie.

Photo Credits

Norvia Behling: 22, 38, 40, 88, and 145; Kent Dannen: ix, 3, 6, 8, 9, 11, 14, 20, 23, 24, 33, 34, 46, 49, 53, 59, 66 (top), 74, and 125; Tara Darling: 10, 13, 17, 30, 47, 66 (bottom), 67, 70, 71, 72 (bottom), 75, 80, 94, 96, 97, 99, 101, 103, 104, 106, 110, 113, 118, and 131; Cheryl Ertelt: 4, 5, 21, 39, 127, and 140; Isabelle Francais: xii, 15, 27, 35, 37, 41, 44, 45 (top and bottom), 48, 50, 51, 52, 56, 57, 63, 65, 72 (top), 81, 84, 89, 92, 108, 133, 138, 142, and 146; and Pets by Paulette: 68, 134, and 143.

All inquiries should be addressed to:
Barron's Educational Series, Inc.
250 Wireless Boulevard
Hauppauge, NY 11788
www.barronseduc.com

Library of Congress Catalog Card No. 2005053031
ISBN-13: 978-0-7641-3309-1
ISBN-10: 0-7641-3309-8

Library of Congress Cataloging-in-Publication Data
Stahlkuppe, Joe.
   Training your pit bull / Joe Stahlkuppe.
     p. cm.
   Includes bibliographical references (p.) and index.
   ISBN-13: 978-0-7641-3309-1 (alk. paper)
   ISBN-10: 0-7641-3309-8 (alk. paper)
   1. Pit bull terriers—Training. 2. Pit bull terriers—
Behavior. I. Title.

SF429.P58S73   2006
636.755′935—dc22   2005053031

Printed in China
9 8 7 6 5

Acknowledgments

For any book project there are always many contributors and consultants that help flesh out the writer's basic framework. There are many such individuals for this book. Diane Jessup provided keen insights (through her web site and her own books) into the psyche of the Pit Bull. Other experts have been included in the "Useful Addresses, Web Sites and Literature" section.

For their immeasurable help in providing a wide platform of listeners for the concepts inculcated in this book, I want to dedicate it to the students at Gardendale High School, Gardendale Elementary School, West Jefferson Elementary School, Bragg Middle School, and Bottenfield Middle School. Their suggestions are to be seen throughout this effort.

I want to thank David Rodman for his keen editorial insights at Barron's and my wife Cathie for her tremendous help in preparing this book. I also want to acknowledge my son, Shawn, and his wife, Lisa, and my four grandchildren, Catie, Peter, Julia, and Alexandra, for their patience and love in dealing with a single-minded grandfather–writer.

Cover Credits

Cheryl Ertelt: front cover; Isabelle Francais: inside front cover; and Karen Hudson: back cover and inside back cover.

Important Note

This book tells the reader how to train a Pit Bull. The author and publisher consider it important to point out that the advice given in the book is meant primarily for normally developed puppies and adult dogs from a good breeder—that is, dogs of excellent physical health and good character.

Anyone who adopts a fully grown dog should be aware that it has already formed its basic impressions of people. There are dogs that, as a result of bad experiences with people, behave in an unnatural manner or may even bite. Only people that have experience with dogs should take in such an animal.

Even well-behaved dogs sometimes do damage to someone else's property or cause accidents. It is, therefore, in the owner's interest to be adequately insured against such eventualities, and we strongly urge all dog owners to purchase a liability policy that covers their dogs.

Contents

3 Pit Bull Positives 19

4 Owning a Pit Bull 28

13 Polishing Your Pit Bull: Beyond the Basics 130

Useful Addresses, Web Sites, and Literature 139

Index 144

Preface

To paraphrase Winston Churchill, *"The Pit Bull is a riddle wrapped in a mystery inside an enigma."* Never has there been a more misunderstood type of dog. Its oldest friends and most famous breeders want to fight it viciously in a pit and its rescuers often end up euthanizing it, perhaps to save the Pit Bull from itself.

Let's get a couple of things straight from the very beginning with two basic truths about Pit Bulls:

1. The Pit Bull does not have to be trained to fight. Aggressiveness toward other dogs is, to one degree or another, an inbred characteristic in most Pit Bulls.
2. While this aggressive nature toward other dogs varies from Pit Bull to Pit Bull, it cannot be corrected by training. Any book or individual that does not acknowledge these two immutable truths about the Pit Bull is incorrect and shows very little understanding of this very special kind of dog.

Throughout their long and storied existence Pit Bulls have shown themselves, except around other animals, to be among the very best of canine companions. Modern bad breeding notwithstanding, the properly bred, properly socialized, and properly trained Pit Bull is a dog the stuff of which family legends are made. Loyal, courageous, strong, and loving of its human family, the Pit Bull has, in the hands of the right owner, the capacity to

There is no need to put the Pit Bull on a pedestal; its qualities speak for themselves.

be the very best dog anyone could ever hope to own.

The wrong dog in the wrong hands is another story altogether. Much of the bad press and bad reputation that afflicts the Pit Bull today comes just from a poorly bred, poorly socialized, poorly trained dog in the hands of a poorly prepared, poorly taught, and poorly motivated owner. Given that a high percentage of people who set out to own a Pit Bull do so for the wrong reasons, it seems only plausible that the statement can be made that there are probably more bad owners of Pit Bulls than there are bad owners of any other breed.

Several kindred breeds continue to be referred to as "Pit Bulls." These breeds include the American Pit Bull Terrier, the American Staffordshire Terrier, the Staffordshire Bull Terrier, the Bull Terrier (White), the Bull Terrier (Colored), and the Miniature Bull Terrier.

Is there no hope? Yes, there is a great deal of hope for the Pit Bull and the right kind of person who seeks to bring such a dog into the family. This hope needs to be built on realistic expectations. This is hope, not hype. Realistic expectations do not come from the kind of dog "knowledge" that one gains from people seeking to sell dogs. The "breed for greed" crowd has only a financial agenda that doesn't care what happens to the buyer or the dog after the business transaction is completed.

It is also true to say that realism does not come from well-modulated announcers' voices coming over the loud speakers at televised dog shows. These faceless voices spew sugar-sweet nonsense about how this or that breed is imbued with almost humanlike characteristics and is perfectly capable of doing what it was originally bred to do. The Pit Bull deserves better than a saccharin-based public relations campaign. The Pit Bull deserves really knowledgeable people taking really knowledgeable approaches to help these potentially wonderful dogs be the best canine companions possible.

Breed Bans

No preface to a book about the Pit Bull would be complete without touching on the insidious cancer of breed-specific legislation (BSL). Three great perils face the Pit Bull (and dogs in general):

1. The underground dog fighters who still exist in the thousands.
2. The radical animal rights groups who would skip inanely from kennel to

Other diverse breeds (and mixtures of these breeds) are often misidentified as "Pit Bulls." Among these are the Bull Mastiff, the American Bulldog, the Great Dane, the Boston Terrier, the Rhodesian Ridgeback, and the Yellow Labrador Retriever.

kennel to free the "poor imprisoned animals" while espousing bans that are a perpetual death penalty on any dog identified as a "Pit Bull."

3. Hype-driven, misdirected, and ineffective banning of breeds.

Breed bans don't work! Such inane, profane, and insane legislation merely shifts the focus of public ire and indignation from one breed to the next breed that will, sooner or later, seem guilty.

This book is about training Pit Bulls. It also addresses dog attacks, fatal and otherwise. Much can be said about train-ing dogs, but perhaps no phrase says it more succinctly than the title of the old standard book by Blanche Saunders, *Training You to Train Your Dog.* There is great truth in this title for there is much to learn because there is much to teach.

■ You should learn that Pit Bulls have many good things to offer dog owners.
■ You should learn the various things that cause dog bites (of which the dog is only one part).
■ You and your entire family should learn how to avoid dog bites and know how to react if a bite occurs.

- You should learn how to be a responsible dog owner and how you and your Pit Bull can be good ambassadors for a grossly maligned breed.

Training Your Pit Bull may not have all the answers about Pit Bull training, but hopefully it will provide an atmosphere for asking the right questions and following the right path. An important part of this book is the section for *Useful Addresses, Web Sites, and Literature.* You are encouraged to dive into this wealth of Pit Bull information for, in the final analysis, the breadth and depth of your knowledge will be your greatest aid in effectively training and responsibly owning your Pit Bull.

The breeds that have been lumped together under the generic name "Pit Bull" constitute some of the very best and very worst of all canines.

1

Presenting the Pit Bull

Profiling the Pit Bull

Many people think they know all there is to know about the type of dog identified as a "Pit Bull." They may have heard about this kind of dog in a news account, on radio, or television. Perhaps they read something about a "Pit Bull" in a newspaper or magazine. Some people may have seen a dog fitting this description. Others may even have read a book about the "Pit Bull." Still others have heard stories about dogs identified as "Pit Bulls."

The fact remains that there is a wide chasm between what the average citizen thinks and assumes about this kind of dog and the truth. Never in the history of dog ownership has so much information and misinformation been so available to so many as in the case of the dog called a "Pit Bull."

People wanting to know about this type of dog often have to wade through the bad press, the hysterical stories and thinly veiled accounts about dogfighting and dogfight adherents. This book does not whitewash this kind of dog, nor is it written solely from a dog show mentality where appearance sometimes matters

more than substance. The focus of this book is on *Training Your Pit Bull.* This is not a generic book on dog training where all one has to make use of it is to change the name of the breed on the cover to make it applicable to each and every breed. This book is about a very specific kind of dog, a dog so tarred by the brush of bad public opinion that the very name has become a catch phrase for "dangerous," "ruthless," and "vicious."

Picking the Name "Pit Bull"

I have decided to appropriate the broad-spectrum name by which many of these dogs are known—"Pit Bull." Many writers and dog experts will correctly tell you that there is no such breed as a "Pit Bull." They are absolutely right in that there is no *specific* breed known simply as a "Pit Bull." The United Kennel Club (UKC), the American Dog Breeders Association (ADBA), and some other organizations have registries for the American Pit Bull Terrier (APBT). The American Kennel Club (AKC) chose a name many decades ago for essentially the same dog as the APBT

Pit Bits: *For generations the dogs we know as Pit Bulls were among the best possible family pets: loyal, friendly, and devoted. Until around 1980 Pit Bull appearances on dog bite statistics were very rare.*

and called theirs first the Staffordshire Terrier and then in the 1970s the AKC changed the name again to the American Staffordshire Terrier (nicknamed Amstaff).

The Kennel Club of England has a popular breed in its registry, the actual ancestor of both the APBT and the Amstaff. This British dog, a bit shorter and smaller than the APBT and the Amstaff, is called the Staffordshire Bull Terrier (nicknamed Staffybull or Staffy). When the AKC accepted the Staffordshire Bull Terrier for registration, the word *American* was appended to the original Staffordshire to become the Amstaff to hopefully avoid confusion between these two breeds. To make things even a little more confusing to the average dog owner, there is the long-faced Bull Terrier (of Spuds McKenzie and Target stores fame) that is, except for its head, shaped very much like the APBT, the Amstaff, and the Staffybull. (The dreaded "Pit Bull" in the movie *Babe: Pig in the City* was actually a Bull Terrier.)

The heritage of the Pit Bull (and the other bull-and-terrier breeds) is clearly defined as a blending of the original Bulldog of England and the now extinct White Terrier (or other related-terriers).

Will the Real Pit Bull Please Stand Up?

As if all these breed names and breed registries weren't confusing enough, the general public and the media often misidentifies any short-haired dog with a somewhat blocky head as a "Pit Bull." Many purebred Boxers and dogs of mixed Boxer ancestry have been branded with the "Pit Bull" stigma. A number of other pure breeds and mongrels are sometimes incorrectly called "Pit Bulls." These dogs, the APBT, the Amstaff, the Staffybull, and some others have also been linked together under the possibly misleading heading of the "bully breeds."

Because of all the confusion with all the names and misidentification, I am going to refer to the dogs that this book is about as Pit Bulls. That is, Pit Bull with a capital "P" and a capital "B." I choose to do this because I want to step across registry lines and over breed boundaries to address training needs of the entire group of dogs that may, rightly or wrongly, be caught up or lumped together in this hodgepodge of hype, headlines, and hysteria.

The Heritage of the Pit Bull

The story of the Pit Bull has its origins with the British bear- and bull-baiting of several centuries ago. In a public square or field varying numbers of dogs were encouraged to attack a chained bull or bear. This activity was called "baiting." While the bear or bull would become enraged, physical damage to them was relatively minor. Conversely, the attacking dogs were often seriously injured or killed. As with most other activities involving dogs, necessity here also became the mother of invention. Mastiffs, the tough, huge hunting and guard dogs of the time, were generally too large and slow to avoid injury or death from a maddened bear or bull. Other breeds of the time proved unsuitable because they could not, or would not, take the punishment dealt out by the much larger opponent.

The First "Bull Dogs"

Gradually, the fans of these brutal contests saw the need for one of the first canine specialist breeds. They produced a smaller and more agile dog and still kept

Perhaps more than any other breed of dog, the Pit Bull has faced many obstacles.

the toughness of the Mastiff. These were the bull-baiting dogs that became "bull dogs." These "bull dogs" were strong, quick, and courageous in attacking an opponent that outweighed them many times over. Because bull-baiting was more common than bear-baiting, these dogs kept the name "bull dog." Portraits of famous "bull dogs" of the period show them to be very similar in size and body shape to the APBT, Amstaff, and Bull Terrier of today. The face and head of these early "bull dogs" was different from the later Pit Bulls in that they had blunt, pushed-in faces with marked underbites.

3

The real Pit Bull has all the qualities to be an excellent pet and companion animal, which belies its reputation as a canine monster.

These animal-on-animal fights by attrition weeded out the slow and the cowardly and left a staunch and rugged competitor.

Note: The short, broad, pushed-in-faced modern Bulldog of the American Kennel Club and the British Kennel Club (generally miscalled the "*English*" Bulldog) is quite a different from the "bull dogs" that battled bears and bulls for public amusement.

Out of Work

Finally, when the British Crown outlawed bull- and bear-baiting, these "bull dogs" were out of work; they had been specifically bred for this one task. While some of them probably transitioned into watch-dogs and the like, there was no task left for these dogs to do. The owners of these "bull dogs" suddenly had lost both the purpose for their dogs and their source of income. Other than the few specimens that would become the ancestors of the modern Bulldog, the bull- and bear-baiting canines became a glut on the market. While some illegal and clandestine battles with bears or bulls may have continued for a time, some of the owners began to look around for a new source of amusement and way to use their bull dogs. The answer they arrived at was fairly obvious—to pit one dog against another.

The Birth of Pit Dogfighting

With bull-baiting gone, dogfighting became more popular, more structured, and more lucrative to the gambling crowd. Dogfighting didn't require the large areas that bull- and bear-baiting needed. Gone were the dangerous bulls and bears; dogfights were easier to conduct and easier to control. Dog pits were usually inside and spectators could be charged an admission fee.

Initially, an attempt was made to simply shift the gritty "bull dogs" over from attacking bears and bulls to fighting each other. "Bull dogs" probably did fight each other, but it was soon realized that the dog needed for baiting was not the dog

This well-bred and well-trained Pit Bull is as good a canine companion as any dog of any other breed, and perhaps better than most.

needed for the dog pits. "Bull dog" fights were not fast enough or with enough action to satisfy an easily jaded gambling and spectator crowd. As with the specialized need for baiting dogs, the dog breeders strove to make bull dogs better suited for the pit. They obviously needed an infusion from somewhere to turn the "bull dogs" into "pit dogs." The answer was not long in coming in the form of another predominantly British kind of dog.

The Terriers

There was another tough and popular kind of dog in the British Isles at the same time dogfighting was beginning—the terriers. These dogs were bred to go deep into the burrows of foxes, badgers, and other animals and drive them out to the hunters waiting aboveground. These terriers were a scrappy group of specialists that could tangle with prey, often much larger than themselves, and survive. Other terriers were fast enough to kill dozens of rats in rat-killing contests. Terriers were fast, flashy, and tough. They were just as gritty or game (willing to fight on and on, even if injured) as were the "bull dogs."

The originators of pit dogfighting had to be aware of the terriers—some dog pits had even been used for "rat killings" by terriers. Terriers were a known entity to the dogfight crowd. The pit breeders recognized terriers as a readily available

Pit Bulls are most often very devoted while being mischievous and clownish.

The Bull-and-Terrier Dogs

Gradually as the "bull dogs" were crossed with various types of terriers, the dog-fighting crowd soon had tough, strong, and fast "bull-and-terriers." It would be this new type of dog that became the pit dog that would ultimately become the Pit Bull of today. Even though there are repeated references to this cross in many British sources, this infusion of terrier into the old "bull dogs" is not accepted by everyone, even to this day. Well-known author of books on the history of dog-fighting and fighting dogs, Richard Stratton points out that many of the old line dogfighting fans in the United States today still refuse to admit that there is *any* terrier ancestry in the pit dogs. Believing that the "bull dogs" from the bear-baiting and bull-baiting days have remained unchanged and have no terrier heritage at all, Stratton and others refer to Pit Bulls as simply "bulldogs."

After considerable research on the origins of the Pit Bull, I don't agree with this view. The terriers of England, Ireland, Scotland, and Wales were (and are) too obvious a source of speed and aggressiveness to not play some role in the molding of the Pit Bull. I base my findings on the fact that the roles of the bull-baiters and the pit dogs are too dissimilar to make any one kind of dog excel at both activi-

solution to the need for speed; the dash, daring, and independent spirit of the terriers was amalgamated with the old bear- and bull-baiting dogs to create a new kind of dog—the "bull-and-terrier."

Pit Bits: *There is, in truth, no actual breed named "Pit Bull." For this book, we have chosen to use this nomenclature to identify all the breeds and breed mixtures that have been lumped together by an uninformed public, ignorant dog owners, and ineffectual lawmakers intent on breed-specific legislation.*

ties. In the baiting of bulls and bears generally, several dogs were in action at the same time. The Pit Bull was designed not as a pack dog, but as a solitary combatant against another solitary combatant. One of the training maxims that is incontrovertible about the Pit Bull is that *you can never trust such a dog not to fight with another dog.*

The End Result

Regardless of the motivations and exact mixtures used by the early dogfighting advocates, they found what they were seeking in the Pit Bull. Perhaps by design or perhaps by luck (or most probably a mixture of both), the early breeders of the "bull-and-terriers" succeeded in creating the best fighting dog, pound for pound, that has ever existed. Jack London, in his classic novel, *White Fang*, has a wolf-dog mixture triumph many times in the dogfighting pit over many kinds of dogs. White Fang won every fight until he is matched with a "bull dog," which was in fact a Pit Bull.

Unlike some others, I will not tout the supposed virtues of the dog pit and of the activity of dogfighting. Dogfighting has now justifiably become a felony in each state of the United States. I have heard Pit Bull breeders talk about how much the dogs enjoy fighting and how such obvious enjoyment could not be cruel. They also like to speak about their role in "keeping the breed alive" and that modern people just don't understand them. I will counter the entire dogfighting crowd's self-promotion by simply pointing out that

Its background notwithstanding, the Pit Bull both historically and now makes an excellent family pet for the right family.

dogfighting began, continued, and remains because people like to bet on the outcomes. One doesn't have to look too closely at gamblers to know that their ultimate goal is not the perpetuation of a noble breed; their goal was, and is, an activity where wagers can be placed. Were it not for the gambling element, dogfighting would have probably disappeared long ago.

This Pit Bull is taking a leisurely sunbath while keeping an alert eye for any opportunities for fun and games with its owner.

Pondering the Pit Bull

To understand the Pit Bull one must understand the environment from which it sprang. Dogfighters developed along with the fighting dogs. Rules and procedures were put in place to ensure a "fair" match, but were probably developed as a way to attract more of the betting public. Dog pits sprang up all over Britain so that dogfighting would be accessible to everyone.

In Britain, and later in the United States, all aspects of dogfighting became cottage industries in some places. Staffordshire, in England's mining country, became so identified with fighting dogs that both the Staffordshire Bull Terrier and the American Staffordshire have monikers that reflect this. The dogfighting fraternity was then, and is now, very clannish and stratified. Not just anyone could buy a Pit Bull puppy from some of the better-known breeders. Not just anyone would be allowed to visit the dog yards of some of the well-known names in the game. Feeding and exercise regimens were kept secret.

Over the many decades that dogfighting flourished, training routines and other methods of getting the most fight out of a Pit Bull developed. Because gambling was such a key part of this blood sport, some dogs were spirited away to remote or inaccessible locations so that they wouldn't become the targets of poison or some other sabotage that might affect the outcome of a match.

Coming to America

Interestingly, the style of the British pits and breeders was adopted and adapted to the New World. Many of the same habits and doings of the British became the same habits and doings of the Americans. Immigration brought many people from England, Scotland, Ireland, and Wales to the United States. With these immigrants came their dogs and their expertise in conducting dogfights.

Dog pit custom and practice can shed some light on the pit dogs themselves. It is important to remember that Pit Bulls had to be safe around humans. It is absolutely wrong to assume that the best fighting dogs were vicious and uncontrollable canine monsters. In the way dogfights were structured, human beings had to handle the dogs in and around the dog pit. A savage dog would be a dangerous liability to its owner, the owner of its opponent, the seconds, and the judges.

Because of the potential for "doctoring" a dog's coat with some bitter-tasting or even poisonous liquid that would affect the biting from the other dog, each Pit Bull was washed, in full view of the crowd, before the fight began. To make sure that the dog was really washed, each dog owner would turn his fighter over to a representative (or "second") affiliated with the other dog's owner for this washing. Imagine what would have happened if Pit Bulls were not trustworthy around strangers!

Many people do not know that, much as in human pugilism, the dogfighters could have a break in the fight to provide simple cooling off and other permitted

All canines show some aggressive behavior, but it has only been in the pit dog breeds that aggression toward other dogs has been brought to the highest extreme.

ministrations to keep a badly hurt dog fighting. Most people in the general public know that it is not safe to approach an injured dog; yet, that is just what the Pit

produce offspring that might have similar bad temperaments.

Richard Stratton, who knows more about fighting dogs and dogfights than probably any other writer today, uses this lack of human aggressiveness in Pit Bulls (from dogfighting families or strains) to state that he believes that such dogs are safer than any other breed around people. I believe that Stratton, at one time, may have been right but that time was when the Pit Bull was from old-time fighting bloodlines. I believe he would agree with me that some of the dogs passed off today as Pit Bulls are not safe around humans.

Puppies learn aggressive tendencies from their littermates. These Pit Bull puppies can still be effectively moved away from hyper-aggressive behavior as adults.

Bull's owner would do when needed and allowed during a dogfight. Imagine if a Pit Bull didn't have a stable temperament. Think of the danger of trying to handle an injured dog that was still affected by the heat of battle!

Kinds of Aggression

While I find dogfighting repugnant and a pastime often enjoyed by people with callous hearts and an even more callous regard for their dogs, I do believe one fact is clear: A fighting dog could not be aggressive toward human beings and survive. It was common practice to kill off any dogs that were vicious and untrustworthy. It also should go without saying that such dogs would never be allowed to

Pit Bulls and Their Plight

Unfortunately, today's Pit Bulls are more likely to have bad temperaments due to a background of bad breeding. The old-line dogfighters, as repulsive as I believe they were, did have dogs that were safe around humans. However, many modern Pit Bull breeders don't have dogs that can be considered safe around other dogs or safe around people. In an ironic twist of fate, old-time breeding for the dog pit made for safer dogs around human beings.

I refer to the "old line" Pit Bull breeders as those who probably have gained their expertise from actual pit dogfighting or from someone else who had that actual dogfighting experience. With all their obvious character flaws, many of these old-liners are not guilty of many of the bad breeding problems seen in Pit Bulls today. Many of the old "names" in dogfighting lore are dead now or have gotten too old to be much of a factor.

Others to whom pit dogfighting has been a vocation or an avocation have smartened up and quit. Some others have attempted to keep personal "pit" reputations, gained in dogfighting, alive under the guise of being "just Pit Bull breeders." Many of the people who continue to fight dogs or breed Pit Bulls for sale as fighters, either in the United States or abroad, are now confronted with laws that make such activities felonies punishable by some significant fines and some serious jail time.

Pit Bulls Today

Today, Pit Bulls are sometimes owned by drug dealers, street punks, "gang-bangers," and common thugs. Many of these Pit Bulls couldn't pass the temperament test of not being human-aggressive. Many of these dogs are in the hands of people who only want "the meanest, baddest dog on the block." It is sad that some great family pets are being held accountable for the actions of bad dogs and worse people. This is, nevertheless, the plight of the Pit Bull.

Most Pit Bulls

We are seeing revisionist history being put forth as truth. Most Pit Bulls never fought in a pit. Most Pit Bulls are not aggressive toward humans and can be controlled as far as their dog-dog aggressiveness is con-

Some of the very finest Pit Bulls have been adopted from Humane Societies, animal shelters, or Pit Bull rescue organizations.

cerned. Most Pit Bulls are not vicious and are so mellow that their positive history almost seems boring when held up against the hateful invective of people who don't really know much about Pit Bulls and who don't have time for the truth. Most Pit Bulls have never bitten anyone. Most Pit Bulls are clownish and impish in their behavior. Most Pit Bulls have the kind of temperament that many other breeds should have. Most Pit Bulls are loyal and loving, happy homebodies.

This book is about training most Pit Bulls.

2 Pit Bull Popularity and Its Price

At first glance it doesn't seem logical to view popularity as a problem, but for most really knowledgeable dog fans popularity for a dog breed is a curse. Popularity has had a negative effect on a number of breeds. Most reputable dog breed clubs don't mind that their breeds are recognizable or have a good public image. What breed clubs don't want for their breeds is to have them become the next pet fads.

In the midst of the storms of current popularity abides the Pit Bull. Perhaps more than any of the other breeds that have endured popularity, the Pit Bull may ultimately suffer longer and suffer more severely. Coming from a barely known breed to one of extreme popularity in just a few short years has had a profoundly negative effect on the Pit Bull. This effect has been in place for the past couple of decades and there seems to be no end in sight.

Popularity Pummels the Pit Bull

For the first 80 or so years of the twentieth century most people wouldn't have been able to pick a Pit Bull out of a canine lineup. The dogs that most frightened people during that eight-decade span were German Shepherd Dogs, Dobermans, and Chows. Annual dog attack statistics rarely, if ever, mentioned the Pit Bull (by any of its related names) prior to 1980. After 1980 things changed radically for the Pit Bull and for any of the related breeds or types.

Two New Bad Boys on the Block

As the 1970s ended there actually were *two* new bad boys on the block. Relatively unknown by most people in previous years, before the decade of the 80s ended, both of these unpublicized dogs would become first notorious and then infamous. These two breeds were the Rottweiler and the Pit Bull (in any of its incarnations).

At the same time the Pit Bull and the Rottweiler were vying for "scariest dog on the planet," sociologists began to notice a change in societal values. Street gangs that had existed for decades, suddenly began to turn inner cities into urban war zones. Crimes against persons

> **Pit Bits:** *When sudden popularity overtook the Pit Bull the breed suffered and continues to suffer. Popularity has negatively affected many excellent breeds. With popularity, the Pit Bull became the "Bogey-Dog" and a good reputation was ruined by the ill informed and by "monster-dog" hype.*

and personal property showed a dramatic increase.

Perhaps eclipsing the human turmoil this old breed type—the Pit Bull—newly discovered, became—justly or unjustly— an icon for the macho aggressiveness that was storming the country. For a new generation with a new attitude came a dog that seemed to exemplify that attitude— the Pit Bull. Almost overnight the number of Pit Bulls tripled and then tripled again. When asked to explain why he wanted to own a Pit Bull one teenager from a large urban inner city was quoted in a major newspaper as saying, "'Cause I want the baddest dog on my street."

Pit Bulls in Peril

Popularity hit the Pit Bull with tsunami force. These until-now carefully bred dogs owned by perhaps 10,000 or so dogfighters and breed fans rapidly became a status symbol for hundreds of thousands of troubleseekers. The rarely (up to this time) human-aggressive Pit Bull suddenly morphed, at least in the public percep-

tion, into a creature unsafe around humans or animals.

This "villianizing" of a breed took place when the traditional dogfighter's breeding goals—aggression against other dogs—became a sort of free-floating, anything-goes aggression. This radical shift away from the way the Pit Bulls had always been happened in a remarkably short time. Fans of hyperaggressive Pit Bulls bred dogs with this extreme temperament, got together, and bred their dogs together. They then inbred the

Popularity has hurt many breeds over the years, but never has a breed been so threatened by popularity as the Pit Bull.

Amid all the rhetoric and venom, people have sometimes forgotten that the overwhelming majority of Pit Bulls have never bitten anyone or anything other than a dog biscuit.

appeared on the attack list only a few decades before suddenly became a head-liner on the list, in the media, and in the minds of many people.

Not only were there suddenly more Pit Bulls in the general canine population, but these dogs began to attract enormous amounts of attention. Smaller dogs have always, as a group, been the most numer-ous culprits on the list of dogs that bit people. Now the Pit Bull seemed to skew dog bite statistics in ways never before observed. Not only were these dogs large enough to do some real damage, but among the Pit Bull population suddenly there were dogs with bad, uncertain, and downright dangerous temperaments.

To make matters even worse, the Pit Bull had always been fairly varied in size and even in general appearance. If a stray mongrel with short hair and no dis-cernible characteristics of another dog breed bit someone, that stray often became identified as the *dreaded Pit Bull*. Purebred dogs from Boston Terriers to Great Danes (and all sizes and mixtures in between) were labeled Pit Bulls by pan-icky bite victims, uninformed witnesses, and sensation-seeking journalists. The writer's adage about a dog biting a man not being news was turned upside down as a new canine *bogeydog*—the Pit Bull—transformed dog bites into news again.

offspring of these ill-conceived pairings. Not only was the Pit Bull becoming more visible on the streets, but now the Pit Bulls that were being seen were completely unlike the Pit Bulls that have ever been before! These new versions of Pit Bulls took only a few short years to destroy the good reputation that the Pit Bull breeds had enjoyed for more than 100 years!

Pit Bulls and Dog Bite Statistics

One test of the negative nature of the general change in the Pit Bull was its sud-den appearance, heretofore unheard of, on the list of dog attacks on humans. A breed, or breed type, that had never

Fear Breeds Hostility

Sadly, there were enough actual Pit Bull attacks, some of them fatal, to keep the pot of public opinion boiling. I remember being taken to task by the mother of a child whose face bore the scars of a Pit Bull bite for even suggesting in my first book that not all Pit Bulls were to blame for the acts of an aberrant few. Also, because I had pointed out in this same book the actual, factual connection between the American Pit Bull Terrier and the American Staffordshire Terrier, an Amstaff breeder at an AKC show wanted to punch me.

The Pit Bull became an emotional lightning rod for all the negatives about dogs. Richard Stratton, Diane Jessup, and other dog writers have also probably had their share of hate mail and insults for attempting to tell the positive truth about the Pit Bull. I have written books about a dozen other dog breeds and only my books on the Pit Bull have drawn any hostility. There must be something deeply ingrained in the public psyche that is set off simply by the mention of Pit Bulls.

"Pit Bull" as a Brand Name

In a way that may have never happened before, a dog breed type has become a polarizing agent. Like the wolf of history and hysteria, and like the "Great White Shark," the words "Pit Bull" have taken on a life of their own. When was the last time that you heard an attorney referred to as "That guy's a real Doberman!" I know a number of attorneys who actually like having the rep of being "a real Pit Bull." Anytime someone has a product that

Caught up in all the furor surrounding the Pit Bull is the jaunty, little Staffordshire Bull Terrier, one of the most popular dog breeds in Britain.

needs a gutsy-tough nickname, it often becomes "the Pit Bull of the industry."

There are now dozens of products that have Pit Bull somewhere in their name or in their description. Everything from heavy-duty cleaning agents to a type of jack used for industrial purposes have taken on the nomenclature of Pit Bull to convey toughness or aggressiveness. I have been a dog fan for over half a century and I know of no other breed of dog that has had its name used in so many

Both the image and the name of the Pit Bull have become marketing magic for many products, and even some goods and services.

applications, most of them with a negative valence.

Popularity's Effect on Breed Quality

One absolute always occurs when a breed or type of dog becomes extremely popular: The overall quality of the dogs in that breed or type decreases. Interestingly, while the total quality of the breed is diminished, the demand for that breed greatly increases. Great demand attracts what I call "the breed for greed crowd." When a breed becomes highly desirable there will always be some puppy mill or backyard novice to meet that desire. This has been the case with many breeds in the past several decades, but this effect has been disastrous on the Pit Bull.

The "breed for greed" bunch is geared up to put out the maximum amount of puppies (or older dogs) of minimum qual-

ity for maximum cash in the quickest time possible. These scoundrels don't care about the dogs they mate together, the offspring of those dogs, or the people to whom those offspring are marketed. They want only a quick money return. If I had my way, every time one of those badly bred Pit Bulls attacks someone, I would charge the greed/breeders as accessories *before* the fact. Some of these Pit Bull outlets may not know any better, but *none* of them really care.

Pit Bulls Produced by Popularity

Some of these would-be "dog breeders" mate brothers and sisters, fathers and daughters, mothers and sons simply because they are available for breeding. Close inbreeding of poor-quality specimens *never* produces a good dog. When the poor quality of dogs concerns their temperament, sooner or later, someone is going to be bitten. According to statistics from the Centers for Disease Control in Atlanta, Georgia, that someone is most often a child. That child may even be from the dog's own family. A bite victim can also be a child who is a relative, a friend, or a neighbor of a dog-owning family. Elderly persons are also in a high-risk category for dog bites.

Most dog bites, including those to children and older people, are of course done by all dogs that are not Pit Bulls! Unfortunately, it is true that the Pit Bull breeds (and dogs identified or misidentified as Pit Bulls) seem to be alternating with the Rottweiler in holding down the top spot for most dog bite attacks, especially the most serious or fatal attacks, by a specific kind or breed of dog.

Pulling the Plug on Dog Bites

Any dog bites are too many dog bites. For those who really want to help the Pit Bull breeds, the best course of action is obvious: Do whatever it takes through education, spaying and neutering, adequate socialization, thorough training, and responsible dog ownership to get the Pit Bull off the top of the list of dogs that bite! It can be done, because it was done for the first 80 years of the twentieth century. Breed bans can't do it, but the people who say they really care about the Pit Bull can!

The average dog buyer mistakenly assumes that every cute and cuddly puppy will grow up to be a reasonably good representative of a particular breed. Buyers of some breeds, especially of the toy varieties, may not be in great physical jeopardy if their pet bites them, but buyers of poorly bred Pit Bull puppies can be. An unpredictable Pit Bull is tantamount to a canine loaded gun brought into the unsuspecting and ill-prepared home.

Bigger Isn't Better

The size factor clearly illustrates another problem of popularity: What the dog-buying public wants, the dog-buying public gets. If the demand is for a Pit Bull that is almost three times the size of the origi-

Not all Pit Bull litters produce alert and highly trainable puppies like this one. Some litters, especially those from poorly bred and potentially aggressive breeding stock, result in potentially dangerous offspring.

nal breed, then the greed/breeders will do whatever is necessary to breed *giant* Pit Bulls. The fact that these huge Pit Bulls could never do what the breed was originally bred to do never seems to dawn on either the buyers or the sellers.

Unfortunately for the Pit Bull reputation and for many ignorant dog buyers, this worst-case scenario has been replicated over and over again. Look in the classified ads section of any major city newspaper and there will be plenty of Pit Bulls for sale. You can get any color you want and even some ads touting "red-nosed dogs"—a famous old-time strain of pit dogs that has probably legitimately ceased to be available some years ago and certainly not to someone outside of the Pit Bull fraternity. You rarely see anything

Pit Bits: *Many Pit Bull breeders produced dogs with excellent temperaments, yet their dogs were branded by the prejudice that swept over the Pit Bull like a tsunami. Many good breeders, realizing that animal shelters were filling up with Pit Bulls and similar dogs stopped breeding their dogs and selling puppies.*

in these advertisements about good temperament or that the mother and father of the puppies are available on the premises for inspection.

Past Popular into Negative

There are two primary ways to determine if a breed is really too popular for its own good. One way to do this is by observing the numbers of dogs of that breed that end up in Humane Societies and animal shelters. When you begin to see large numbers of a particular kind of dog in adoption agencies, then you can reasonably assume that there are too many of that kind of dogs out in the general population. The equation would go something like this: More dogs available mean that some poor owners will get some of those dogs and upon realizing their mistake, will bring their dogs to the animal shelter.

The second way to recognize a dog breed that has become too popular for its own good is to notice the number of mixed dogs that have a member of that particular breed as one of the parents.

This is called the *Mongrelizing Effect* and it means that more dogs of that breed will wind up in homes where they are not spayed or neutered and perhaps even are allowed to run free in the neighborhood. Unneutered dogs at large in a community will certainly breed with other such dogs as the opportunity presents itself. The resulting puppies are crossbreeds with very little value except as pets. Many of these crossbreeds will end up in poor homes or in animal shelters.

Both of these indicators are true at this time for the Pit Bull. Not only are there many Pit Bulls for sale, there are usually any number of Pit Bulls at animal shelters. While some shelters make a real effort to find good, responsible homes for their Pit Bull adoptees, sometimes they can't and many Pit Bulls are euthanized as a result.

Pit Bull Crosses

There are also many dogs out there of mixed Pit Bull ancestry; in some cases these crossbred Pits are more potentially dangerous than the purebreds. If a Pit Bull is bred to a dog with definite human-aggressive heritage, it is fairly certain that the offspring will be of uncertain and unpredictable temperaments. There has even been a good deal of intentional Pit Bull crossing. Pit Bulls mated with Rottweilers, Bullmastiffs, or American Bulldogs are fairly common. A good rule of thumb is that a mixed Pit Bull will inherit most of the bad attributes of both of its parents. Getting a good purebred Pit Bull is much safer than obtaining an uncertain mixed Pit.

3 *Pit Bull Positives*

The absolute weight of all the negative information circulating about Pit Bulls would have sunk lesser dogs long ago. That there are many good Pit Bulls in the hands of many good owners comes as a great surprise to many of the Pit Bull villifiers and breed ban advocates. Sadly, Pit Bulls have become canine lightning rods, even when they do something good, somebody with an anti-Pit Bull agenda will try to find a way to ignore it, spin it, or negate it.

A major metropolitan newspaper carried a story about a child's pet that saved the child from an attack by a Rottweiler. The newspaper had a happy picture of the hero dog and the rescued toddler. The hero dog was clearly a Pit Bull, but no mention was made of this fact in the article or in the caption under the photo. Just when you want some Pit Bull recognition, it doesn't happen!

On the Plus Side

Pit Bulls are quite capable of doing positively outstanding things. As noted, prior to 1980 there was very little negative information about this type of dog, but unfortunately, since 1980 there have been many bad accounts about Pit Bulls; some of these accounts are justified, but many others are pure hyperbole.

One interesting account of a good deed performed by a Pit Bull comes from a *Parade* magazine article (December 23, 2001). This article was about how actor Ken Howard's life was saved by his American Pit Bull Terrier, Shadow. The incident took place while Howard was in poor health awaiting a kidney transplant. *"My wife and our dog, Shadow, were outside, and I fell on the bathroom floor upstairs, and somehow the dog knew. If he hadn't alerted my wife, I might have bled to death right there."*

Pit Bulls as Heroes

Most Pit Bulls aren't as directly involved with saving their owner's life as was Shadow, but heroic actions are certainly not alien to these dogs. The 1993 Ken-L Ration's Dog Hero of the Year was a Pit Bull named Weela. Weela had a good record as a pet, but made it better when she was credited with helping to save the lives of 30 people, 29 dogs, 13 horses, and even a cat from drowning in a California flood, by leading them through rushing

19

> **Pit Bits:** *Combined with prejudice and ignorance, attacks on humans and on other dogs by imposter or "Quasi-Pits" fueled a fire of human panic that threatens to destroy both good and bad dogs alike.*

waters to safety. Weela repeatedly braved the flood to show safe routes. She later swam back and forth towing food to stranded animals.

Another Pit Bull, Bogart, saved a four-year-old child from drowning in a Florida swimming pool. Dixie, a Georgia Pit Bull,

saved some small children from being bitten by a cottonmouth water moccasin. Sebastian, a Pit Bull, tackled a much larger Rottweiler when it attacked a six-year-old child. Sebastian kept the attacking dog away from the injured child until help arrived.

Though often falsely portrayed as vicious, ruthless canine monsters, many Pit Bulls are service dogs, specially trained to help their physically challenged owners. Spike, a Pit Bull, faithfully serves his owner, a quadriplegic, and allows his owner a more normal chance at life. The Pit Bull was heralded as helping his owner gain a college degree in computer software.

All most Pit Bulls need is an atmosphere where the individual dog is judged on its own merit and not forced into hiding by vicious and unfounded rumor and myth.

Therapeutic Pit Bulls?

The Chako Rescue Association has Pit Bull therapy dogs in Texas, California, and Utah. One hospice organization prefers to use well-mannered Pit Bulls with seniors in nursing homes and assisted living programs. The hospice director was amazed that so many of the older persons with whom she works had once owned or had been around and had fond memories of Pit Bulls as pets from earlier days.

Sacramento, California has a trio of certified SAR (Search and Rescue) Pit Bulls named Cheyenne, Dakota, and Tahoe. So good were the search and rescue efforts of these three, that Dakota was called on to assist as a search dog in the tragic 2003 Space Shuttle disaster. She was also used in the search for murder victim Laci Peterson. It seems that Cheyenne, Dakota, and Tahoe are not only SAR certified, they are true Renaissance dogs. After fulfilling

Both the celebrity and the true character of the Pit Bull has made it popular.

their regular duties, this threesome also became certified hospital therapy dogs!

RCA, a Pit Bull, was Alaska's first certified hearing dog who helped her owner, Donna Lindsay, function more independently. Taylor is another Pit Bull whose role is sniffing out drugs and contraband for the U.S. Customs Service. The number one U.S. Customs Service dog is a Pit Bull named Popsicle. This amazing drug and contraband sniffer dog came by his name in an ironic way. He was found during a drug raid in a freezer where he had been left to die after being used in dog-fighting.

One of the most unusual positive stories is of an Arizona Pit Bull "Pitcasso," also named Taylor, that paints pictures—it is true—that are then auctioned off to benefit charitable organizations. After garbing the dog in a painter's smock, Taylor's owners lay out a variety of colorful paints and a piece of white art paper. Taylor then runs with artistic abandon,

creating paw prints and long sliding lines of an amazing variety of color. Taylor's owners then frame the masterpiece. According to a 2000 issue of the *Arizona Republic*, one of Taylor's paintings sold for $600, which went to the Phoenix Children's Hospital's Leukemia Ward.

Tanner, a tracking and protection Pit Bull with the Cooke County, Tennessee Sheriff's office was so appreciated by his human colleagues that he was awarded a real badge and a real bulletproof vest. Another Tennessee Pit Bull named Leah saved the lives of her human family by alerting them that their home was on fire. Buddy, a Pit Bull, also saved his owner from certain death in a blaze that destroyed their home.

This 13-year-old Amstaff has been a devoted companion to a caring owner.

The classic Pit Bull appearance belies the truth of a happy disposition that makes most Pit Bulls very poor protection animals.

In a Brookfield, Connecticut, housefire, Rover McGuinness, a Pit Bull, woke his owner John Murray who had to jump from a second-story window to avoid burning to death. Murray, a U.S. Army veteran, made it but Rover McGuinness, whose incessant and frantic barking had alerted Murray, was unable to escape and died in the blaze.

Iceberg, a New Jersey Pit Bull was shot while protecting his owner Israel Tavarez from armed assailants. Though seriously wounded, Iceberg gamely kept on coming and the gunmen fled. Emergency surgery, paid for by area animal lovers, saved the brave dog's life. A similar story comes from South Richmond, Virginia. Three ski mask-wearing men smashed in the door of Travis Rappold's apartment. One of the intruders brandished a pistol toward

Rappold and several of his friends. The apparent robbers had not counted on Rock, Rappold's 75-pound Pit Bull, who charged the three criminals. As they ran back out of the shattered door with Rock in hot pursuit, one of the would-be thieves fired a shot hitting Rock in the chest. Rock, a true hero, died in his owner's arms.

A 10-year-old Wichita, Kansas girl was alone at home, sick, from school, when a lone intruder forced his way into the child's house. The man, demanding money, began chasing the terrified little girl. It was at that moment that this thug got more than he bargained for when the family Pit Bull, Coco, attacked him and chased him away.

Chevy, a Canadian Pit Bull, only 10 months old, came to her owner's aid when the woman fell in her home and struck her head. Chevy began barking and ran to another part of the home and got help. In Nebraska, a similar story unfolded when Jessie, a Pit Bull, awoke her owner who had had recent surgery on his arm. The man was asleep and it was the middle of the night. Jessie barked until her owner woke up and turned on a light and saw that he was bleeding profusely. A quick trip to the hospital saved his life.

Pit Bulls have often been blamed for attacks on humans, but sometimes it is the Pit Bulls that stop dog attacks. Anthony Romaro, a Florida seven-year-old was attacked by two 100-pound Akitas. Anthony suffered severe bites to his head and ears. Seeing the attack, a neighbor of the boy released his two-year-old female Pit Bull who attacked the much larger Akitas, allowing adults to rush in and pick up Anthony and transport him to a nearby hospital's emergency room.

Red, White, and Blue Pit Bulls

During World War I, the Pit Bull was used as a tough-as-nails symbol for the American soldier, sailor, and airman. It is interesting to note that America's first dog of war was Stubby, a Pit Bull. Serving with the American troops in World War I, Sergeant Stubby (his actual rank!) was awarded a number of combat medals and is credited with alerting his unit of an impending German gas attack. Stubby was invited, with honors, not once, but three times to the White House.

"Petey the Pup" and Pit Bulls of the Rich and Famous

"Petey the Pup" was the canine babysitter for the popular "Little Rascals" movies. A registered American Pit Bull Terrier in the United Kennel Club, Petey (double-registered) was also one of the first Staffordshire Terriers—later known as *American* Staffordshire Terriers—registered by the American Kennel Club. Petey, with a circle drawn around his left eye, was just the kind of dog that many American children wanted during the 1930s and

This handsome, young Pit Bull is much more likely to become an excellent companion animal if it is properly socialized and carefully trained.

This handsome red-nosed Pit Bull exudes the happy confidence that is a hallmark of these dogs.

1940s. When TV brought the series into America's living rooms, no one thought it odd that a Pit Bull would be a children's pet. The negatives would come later.

The early years of the Pit Bull were years without hype and without wild-eyed extremists calling for breed bans. The Pit Bull was one of the dogs at the top of the list of preferred pets. President Theodore Roosevelt owned one and sang its praises. So much did Silent Cal like Pit Bulls that President Calvin Coolidge had two of them. General George Patton had Willie the Bull Terrier, also called William the Conqueror. President Woodrow Wilson owned a Pit Bull, as did tough-guy actor Humphrey Bogart and his starlet wife Lauren Bacall. Elegant dancer/actor Fred Astaire owned a Pit Bull and so did his friend, Bing Crosby. Boxing greats Jack Dempsey and Jack Johnson were enthusiastic Pit Bull supporters. Before his famous Standard Poodle, Charley, came into his life, author John Steinbeck had a Pit Bull.

Thomas Alva Edison was a Pit Bull owner and took some of the first moving pictures of his dogs. Author and humanitarian, Helen Keller owned a Pit Bull and was not shy in extolling its virtues. The Little Tramp, Charlie Chaplin had a Pit Bull as a pet. Curvaceous French actress, Bridgit Bardot kept company with a Pit Bull.

A large number of modern, human stars have chosen Pit Bulls as their canine companions, among them: Steve Irwin (The Crocodile Hunter); basketball giant Shaquille O'Neal; actor Michael J. Fox; singer Usher; the appropriately named actor Brad Pitt; actor/producer/comedian Mel Brooks and his wife, the late Anne Bancroft; singer/actress/celebrity Madonna; TV star/comedian Ray Romano; actress Alicia Silverstone; commentator Jon Stewart, and many others.

Pit Bulls as War Dogs

Pit Bulls stood by their owners through the Great Depression and when World War II broke out, Pit Bulls were among the first dogs chosen for the newly formed Dogs for Defense. So well did one Pit Bull mix perform that he was bred with an Airedale and produced three noteworthy war dog sons named *GI, OD,* and *BC.*

This trio was legendary for the tough missions they were able to accomplish.

Being military oriented was nothing new for Pit Bulls. One of the most telling pieces of evidence involving the long-time acceptance of Pit Bulls as something special is a Pit Bull named Sallie. In a rare lithograph, a war-weary Sallie is pictured right after a battle. Sallie was the official Regimental Mascot of the 11th Pennsylvania Volunteer Infantry. Like the courageous Pit Bulls that would come after her, Sallie had seen her share of battle. She accompanied her soldier-boys in the Civil War battle at Gettyburg.

> **Pit Bits:** *The real Pit Bull has many of the most wonderful characteristics, traits, and abilities that can be put into any kind of dog. As good as these dogs can be, honestly they are not right for every home or for every dog owner. But in the right setting, under the right circumstances, and with the right humans, the Pit Bull can become one of the greatest of all companion animals.*

Putting Pit Bulls in Perspective

An anti-Pit Bull person might point out that there are many other breeds that have been heroic, done amazing things, or were owned by celebrities. That is certainly true. What makes the Pit Bull different is the fact that most people have never heard about all the good things about these dogs. There were countless other positive accounts than those included here, but reading an endless litany of all the good things done by the Pit Bull breeds would miss the mission of this book on training your Pit Bull.

Because Pit Bulls are constantly being compared with other dogs that don't have the same "baggage" that Pit Bulls have, there needs to be a place of neutral ground where all dogs, regardless of their genetic makeup, can be gauged by objective measurements. That neutral ground is found with the American Temperament Test Society, Inc. (ATTS).

ATTS and Temperament Testing

ATTS is a national, not-for-profit organization "...for the uniform temperament evaluation of purebred and spayed/neutered mixed-breed dogs." In addition to its unbiased temperament testing mandate, ATTS selects, trains, prepares, and registers temperament evaluators and works for the betterment of all breeds of dogs. The organization also disseminates important behavioral information to the public and to dog owners, breeders, and trainers. ATTS recognizes and awards certificates "...to dogs that pass the requirements of the temperament evaluation." The ATTS motto cogently ties all these goals together with the phrase "A Sound Body and a Sound Mind."

Quoting from ATTS material: *"The test takes about 12 minutes to complete. The dog is on a loose 6-foot (1.8-m) lead and three ATTS trained evaluators score the dog. Majority rules. Failure on any part of the test* is recognized *when a dog shows panic, strong avoidance without recovery or unprovoked aggression."* For more of the actual testing information, rules, and locations where tests are to be given, see American Temperament Test Society, Inc. in the Useful Addresses section at the end of this book.

Temperament Testing

When evaluating an individual dog ATTS takes into account the *"breed's temperament, training, health and age..."* The minimum age for testing is 18 months. The rate of passing may differ among the various breeds, but the test is uniformly administered. On average, about 80.9 percent of the dogs that take the test pass. A dog that passes the ATTS earns the TT (Temperament Tested) title.

Representatives of all of the breeds that have been lumped into the Pit Bull nomenclature in this book have been tested. Looking at the latest testing (as of December 2004) some interesting observations will help put the Pit Bull into a proper perspective with all the other breeds.

Pit Bulls and Others

In presenting these numbers, they are given only to show how certain dogs of certain breeds have done in the ATTS evaluation. I am making no statement

that implies that all dogs of a particular breed or any individual dog of any particular breed would do better, worse, or as well as these figures reveal. These figures will merely point out how *some* dogs of *some* breeds did when evaluated fairly and on a common scale. Neither ATTS nor I want to use these findings to say that a particular breed is better than some other breed when it comes to temperament. What is interesting here is that the Pit Bull breeds fall so close to the norm for all dogs that were evaluated by the ATTS evaluators—only that and nothing more.

Temperament Results and Pit Bull Breeds

The name of the breed comes first, then the percentage of dogs that have passed, and then the number of dogs of this breed tested to date. ATTS statistics reveal that:

- 83.3 percent (391 out of 469) of American Pit Bull Terriers have earned the TT certification.
- For American Staffordshire Terriers, 83.4 percent (400 out of 480) passed the test.
- For the American Bulldog the numbers are 81.9 percent (95 out of 116) were certified.
- The Bull Terrier scored 90.9 percent passing (50 out of 55).
- The Miniature Bull Terrier logged 100 percent (7 out of 7).
- The Staffordshire Bull Terrier (Staffy Bull) had a 93.2 percent passing rate (55 out of 59).

Temperament Results and Other Breeds

Solely for limited comparison purposes, I have chosen some other popular breeds, with their ATTS percentages:

- Boxer—84.7 percent (282 out 333)
- Bulldog (miscalled the *English* Bulldog)—68.3 percent (82 out of 120);
- Cocker Spaniel—81.5 percent (176 out of 216)
- Collie—79.0 percent (635 out of 791)
- Doberman Pinscher—76.5 percent (1,070 out of 1,399)
- German Shepherd Dog—82.8 percent (2,250 out of 2,717)
- Golden Retriever—83.6 percent (551 out of 659)
- Great Dane—78.6 percent (180 out of 229)
- Labrador Retriever—91.1 percent (587 out of 644)
- Rottweiller—82.3 percent (3,702 out of 4,498)
- Mixed-Breed Dogs (spayed/neutered)—85.1 percent (579 out of 680)

Reasonable Assumptions

It is reasonable to assume that the average dog of any of these breeds or types might or might not fall within the same percentages. What is worth noting is that dogs that have been identified as Pit Bulls aren't really that different from the other popular breeds that have been touted for their exceptional temperaments. A well-bred, well-socialized, and well-trained American Pit Bull Terrier compared to a

This Staffordshire Bull Terrier (the ancestor of the Pit Bull and the American Staffordshire Terrier, and one of the most popular breeds in Britain) seems to be playfully sticking out her tongue at her detractors.

well-bred, well-socialized, and well-trained Golden Retriever or German Shepherd Dog or Pomeranian should be able to fall within the general parameters of the ATTS evaluation. Some individual dogs may do somewhat better and some individual dogs may do somewhat worse.

The American Temperament Test Society, Inc. performs a valuable service to the world of dogs by making these tests available all over the United States. For a small fee your pet can be tested and you can gain a great insight into the temperament of your dog and what things your training program may need to address.

4 *Owning a Pit Bull*

The Proper Pit Bull Person

Long before you ever own a Pit Bull, hopefully you will have given yourself a realistic test to see if your wants and desires regarding a Pit Bull mesh with your actual lifestyle, personality type, and current situation. Far too many Pit Bulls have come into this world with all they needed to be exceptional human companions only to have their good qualities subverted, their natural tendencies exploited, and their chances for a good home and a long life ruined.

Without a proper personal assessment, you are doing no good for yourself, your family, or for some innocent Pit Bull that

> **Pit Bits:** *The proper Pit Bull person is someone who isn't interested in owning the "meanest dog on the block," doesn't want a dog as a macho fashion accessory, and has enough time and ability to produce the dog from its instinctual behaviors and from a society often out on a canine witch-hunt.*

may have the grave misfortune to come to belong to you. A personal evaluation, done honestly, will be the best thing you can possibly do as far as dog owning is concerned. Combining some hints from the *PitbullLovers.com* Web site and other sources, the following is a test that you can administer to yourself to determine your suitability as a Pit Bull owner.

Think About Your Answers

Before you think that this book is an ax job on Pit Bulls or a personal affront to you, remember that there are thousands upon thousands of Pit Bulls that have been purchased with the finest of intentions only to have them given away, often to the nonexistent "farm in the country," thrown out on an empty stretch of highway, surrendered to the dogcatcher, or placed for adoption at the local animal shelter. The saddest part of all this is that most of these bad outcomes weren't the Pit Bull's fault at all.

Far too many people in almost all the popular breeds are ill prepared personally, financially, and emotionally to own a dog. When that dog is a Pit Bull, the end result is a foregone conclusion and the dog usually dies as a consequence. If there is one thing for certain about Pit Bulls it is that they rarely get a second chance. While some adopted Pit Bulls end up in great families with people who adore them and know how to keep them safe, a great many more end up with dogfighters, chained to a barrel, locked away in some basement, or put to death.

This test is one way that you can realistically assess your capacity as a potential Pit Bull owner. Each question is designed not for someone else to know whether you would be a good person to own a Pit Bull. Each question—and some may seem redundant—has been formulated so that *you* can know for yourself if you and a Pit Bull are a good match.

Many excellent Pit Bull pets are adopted from animal shelters or from canine rescue organizations.

What to Consider If You Want to Own a Pit Bull

Lifestyle

Pit Bulls aren't easy to ignore; they are terriers in every sense of the word, wired for action and ready for fun. A couch potato human being is a poor choice for a Pit Bull owner. In most cases, sedentary people are setting themselves up for failure if they obtain a Pit Bull. Energy and a sense of humor—Pit Bulls are among the most humorous of dogs to own—are prerequisites for successful ownership.

A lifestyle that leaves little else after getting out of bed, going to work, coming home from work, going to bed, and starting this cycle over and over again would not be a good fit for a Pit Bull. One of the reasons that some Pit Bulls get into trouble is that their owners haven't spent enough time with them. This is a very hands-on, time-requiring, high-maintenance (from an emotional viewpoint) breed. If your schedule is taut or full, do everyone a favor and pass on the Pit Bull.

A lifestyle filled with the comings and goings of strangers, especially children that haven't been schooled on how to act around dogs, is a bad place for a Pit Bull. Most dog bites (of all breeds and types of dogs) occur to children under 15 years old, at their own home, at the home of a neighbor, or at the home of a relative. While Pit Bulls can be great with children, they (both children *and* dogs) need a lot of supervision, which requires a lifestyle where that supervision can readily be provided.

Home Schooling

Should I Own a Pit Bull?

I. What About My Lifestyle and a Pit Bull?

A. Many Pit Bulls are high-octane canines. How does that fit with my personality?

B. Does my lifestyle coincide with a super-energetic pet?

C. Knowing that a tired Pit Bull is a happy Pit Bull, do I have the energy that owning a Pit Bull will require?

Owning a Pit Bull means owning a trained Pit Bull. Every dog deserves to be effectively and consistently trained.

D. Do I have the time to give in my schedule that a Pit Bull will require and deserve?

E. Am I the only one to consider or does my life include a family and close friends that may or may not mesh well with a Pit Bull?

F. Is my lifestyle constant or is there a potential for a change that might not work out well for a Pit Bull?

G. Does my lifestyle cause me to travel, which would necessitate leaving my Pit Bull behind?

H. Have I so many interests that a Pit Bull might not get my full attention?

I. Does my lifestyle include lots of other people and other pets?

II. What About My Budget and a Pit Bull?

A. Can I afford to get the best possible Pit Bull?

B. Do I have enough cash reserves for proper veterinary care for my Pit Bull?

C. Can I take time away from work to get my Pit Bull immediate medical care, should it be needed?

D. Do I have enough money for collars, leads, crates, toys, and all the other supplies that a Pit Bull should have or will need?

E. Does my budget have enough leeway for a professional trainer or for perhaps extended training classes?

F. Can I afford to feed the best-quality dog food for my Pit Bull?

G. Could I keep up with my Pit Bull's needs if I lost my job or suffered financial reverses?

H. Will I have the resources if my home-owner's insurance goes up due to my owning a Pit Bull?

III. What About My Environment and a Pit Bull?

A. Does my home, apartment, condo have enough room for a Pit Bull?

B. Do I understand that my Pit Bull should absolutely live in my home with me?

C. Is where I live conducive to a comfortable existence for a Pit Bull?

D. If I have a yard, is it securely fenced and is it a safe place for a Pit Bull to be?

E. Do I know that Pit Bulls are among the dogs most often stolen?

F. If I have a family, how will they react to spending their lives 24/7 with a Pit Bull that will require a certain amount of care and ample attention?

IV. What About My Real Motivation in Owning a Pit Bull?

A. Do I want to own a Pit Bull to impress other people?

B. Have I ever pictured in my mind how I would look walking down the street with a Pit Bull?

C. Do I hunger for the toughest dog on my street?

D. Do I have a need for a Pit Bull to be a protection animal?

E. Would my ego get a boost if I owned a Pit Bull?

V. What About My Experience with Dogs in General?

A. Would a Pit Bull be my first dog?

B. Have I ever dealt with a large, possibly aggressive dog?

C. Have I ever trained a dog?

D. Have I ever owned a Pit Bull that turned out to be a poor choice of pets?

E. Do I have a proven track record as a responsible dog owner?

F. Have I ever been to a dog show, an obedience trial, or a dog training class?

G. If I owned a Pit Bull, does my family understand enough about dog training to not undo all the training I might do?

VI. Am I Emotionally Equipped to Own a Pit Bull?

A. Can I avoid becoming frustrated and angry with my Pit Bull if things don't go quite as I envisioned them?

B. Do I have enough emotional maturity to keep my Pit Bull (and myself) out of trouble?

C. Do I have a great deal of patience?

D. Am I consistent or am I more prone to impulsive behavior?

E. Would I be able to handle the potential alienation of some friends and acquaintances due to my owning a Pit Bull?

F. Would I be able to keep from becoming angry and doing something rash if someone insulted (or worse) me and my Pit Bull?

Most dog experts believe that the quality of the dog as a pet is usually reflected in the caring and awareness of the dog's owners. This is especially true for the Pit Bull.

Pit Bulls are really people-oriented dogs. Always having to board them at the veterinarian's or put them up with friends or relatives presents a real hardship on this kind of dog. Such arrangements, especially with friends and family members, run the risk of the Pit Bull getting into trouble. Travel if you must, but take your pet with you; be sure to check laws in the places you may be visiting as some locales can confiscate your Pit Bull and euthanize it solely because it is a Pit Bull or looks like a Pit Bull.

If your life is in a constant state of flux and you aren't sure where you will be living next month, a Pit Bull is not right for you. Dogs are much more attuned to their surroundings than we might want to believe. Usual sights, scents, and sounds are a comfort and come to be expected. Different locations tend to keep some dogs always on the defensive because

they never really know where or what their territory is.

If you have a lot of hobbies and interests, a Pit Bull may not be right for you. This is a living, breathing creature that will come to adore you. If you have so much going on that the Pit Bull can't be one of your highest priorities, do an innocent dog a favor and don't buy or adopt it. Look at your lifestyle, then look at the Pit Bull. If the two aren't a match, then don't bring a dog into a way of living that won't work out best for the dog (or you).

Budget

Dog owning done correctly is a fairly expensive proposition. If you try to buy a Pit Bull puppy, for example, you definitely don't want any with bargain-basement price tags. A good Pit Bull from a good genetic background is always your best option. That is not to say that an adoption dog might not do well, but even then you may face a variety of expenses.

Expenses

Veterinary visits, a strong fence—make that 6 feet (1.8 m) tall or more and set far enough into the ground to keep an avid digger in—a kennel, a crate, tough dog chew toys, and a variety of other things will cost you money. Some insurance companies won't care about how innocent and cute your Pit Bull is and they may increase your premiums.

Top-quality dog food and the right kind of dog treats will be an ongoing budgetary item. Using a good professional trainer will be money well spent, but it will still be money spent. While a Pit Bull doesn't require all the *frou-frou* grooming that some breeds do, the dog will still deserve the things it needs and it is unwise to try to "cheap out" if you want a good and healthy Pit Bull pet.

Motivation

The reason you want a Pit Bull may be the most important aspect of your personal Pit Bull ownership assessment. If you need a dog to make you feel more secure, more macho, more attractive to the opposite sex, more dignified, more impressive or any other shallow motivation, you don't need a Pit Bull. If any of these is your real reason for wanting a Pit Bull, you may want to talk to a counselor.

If you want the toughest dog on your block as a status symbol, then you have more problems than just the lack of a dog. Pit Bulls aren't like pistols to be brandished or waved around. Pit Bulls can certainly handle themselves against many kinds of foes, but when a Pit Bull has to do that, it generally is a sign of a bad owner. It is also true that the Pit Bull that has to fight for any reason is also much more likely to be ultimately euthanized as a danger to himself and to the community.

Pit Bulls may seem to be the ideal protection dog, but they aren't—far from it. Most Pit Bulls are so human-oriented that they will meekly walk away with anyone who gives them a kind word and hooks a leash on their collar. In my book, *The American Pit Bull Terrier Handbook,* I gave the illustration of a man who owned several Pit Bulls that he kept in separate ken-

A good Pit Bull is a controlled Pit Bull. A controlled Pit Bull is on a leash or in a fenced backyard and never allowed to run freely in a neighborhood!

nels in his backyard. This man had to put a fence around the entire kennel area and buy a guard dog (of another, more protective breed) to keep people from stealing his Pit Bulls!

Leave your ego out of any decision to buy any kind of a dog, but most especially a Pit Bull. They can be great dogs. They can be impressive dogs. They can be courageous dogs. They can also be the wrong dogs for people with the wrong motivation to own them. Don't confuse owning a good dog with being a good dog owner. Just because you happen to have a good dog (or a potentially good dog) does not mean that you are or will ever be a good dog owner. That takes commitment, sacrifice, and careful planning.

Training a Pit Bull should be a happy experience for both the trainer and the trainee. Viewing dog training as a chore takes all of the fun and most of the effectiveness out of it, for human and canine.

Experience

While some experts differ with me on this point, I believe it is wise not to let your first experience with a dog be with a Pit Bull. It is possible that a neophyte dog owner could do all the homework and all the planning and all the preparation and then become a very successful Pit Bull owner. Unfortunately, the homework, planning, and preparation are not usually what a novice dog owner thinks about and then this person wonders why things turned out so badly with a Pit Bull.

A person who has owned a large and powerful dog and has dealt with the issues that such a dog brings is much more likely to have the proper mindset when

obtaining a Pit Bull. However, it is a mistake to think that just because you had a successful experience with another dog of another breed that you are guaranteed a similar experience with a Pit Bull. Pit Bulls are different from many of the other kinds of dogs. Their fighting dog heritage makes them different.

It is also easier to train a Pit Bull if you have gone through this process with another dog. One of the most successful Pit Bull owners that I know had had a series of Labrador Retrievers before he got a rescue Pit Bull. His experience with the Labs, while it didn't translate perfectly over to the Pit Bull, was enough to help him get a good start as a Pit Bull owner.

Knowledge

One thing that potential Pit Bull owners could and should do, whether they have owned a dog before or not, is to visit a number of dog shows, obedience events, dog training classes, and kennels. Not much can be absorbed strictly by locational osmosis, but talking with as many real dog people as possible can't hurt. There is a list of many books to read and Web sites to visit in the back of this book. One thing is certain about the Pit Bull: the more you know (from whatever the source), the better things will be with you and whatever kind of dog you decide to get.

Emotional Factors

Some people are just not emotionally right for Pit Bulls, or some other breeds as well. A perfectionist who expects immediate gratification will probably become

As with this young Staffordshire Bull Terrier, his mother will be his first teacher. The human trainer must pick up where the dog's mother left off.

very frustrated with Pit Bulls and most other kinds of dogs. Patience isn't just a slogan in regard to a Pit Bull; patience is a mantra that should become an obsession. A person without patience will probably never find any kind of dog—and very few human beings—that will be good enough.

An impulsive person with a Pit Bull is a real problem looking for a place to occur. Pit Bulls and spur-of-the-moment-type personalities can really be a dangerous combination. The person who is not capable of controlling his or her own emotions certainly won't be able to supply the con-

trol that a Pit Bull may need to keep it out of harm's way. Many of the cases of serious or fatal dog bites have as their origin an impulsive human and a poorly trained dog.

Keeping Your Cool

The angry person certainly has no business owning a Pit Bull. Like the perfectionist, the angry individual will almost always place any blame for problems everywhere else but where it belongs—on his or her own shoulders. Being angry with a pet

Socialization of any pet includes introducing the dog or puppy to people that may be very different in age, size, and appearance from the dog's owners.

her friends and neighbors may find the Pit Bull the wrong choice of canine companions. Rightly or wrongly, some people will never be able to look on a Pit Bull with anything other than disdain, fear, and loathing. The person who can't handle these anti-Pit Bull folks is headed for a long hard road that often leads straight to an animal shelter. Pit Bull owners all over the world have had to face personal insults, physical attacks, legal barrages, and the cruelest of conjecture and innuendo. Unless you can develop thick skin, the Pit Bull is not the right dog for you.

that only wants to figure out what you want him to do, and then do it, is the beginning of an abusive relationship. The sad fact is that many of the Pit Bulls that end their lives in animal shelters are often themselves the victims of abuse. Such abuse often stems from being owned by a person whose emotional identity is opposite of what it should be.

The Pit Bull stigma also has its own emotional price tag. Some people are excellent dog owners in all other ways except when it comes to fending off all the hostility that can swirl around a Pit Bull and a Pit Bull owner. The person who desperately wants the approval of his or

The Pit Bull Personality

The other side of this same coin is the person who develops what one pop psychologist has ironically dubbed "a Pit Bull personality." Such an individual walks around with the proverbial "chip on his shoulder." This individual seems to be waiting for someone to say something negative about his or her Pit Bull. When someone obliges this individual—and someone usually will—this person goes into attack mode. One of the strangest examples of this behavior that I have ever heard about involved two men who met while walking their dogs in a city park. One of them owned a Pit Bull; the other had a dog of a different breed. The other owner made a disparaging remark about the Pit Bull owner's dog, something to the effect that such a dog was too vicious to be allowed to live. The Pit Bull owner replied vituperatively in equal hostility.

> **Pit Bits:** *The wrong kind of person for a Pit Bull is an impulsive, neglectful, insecure, thrill-seeker who wants a dog to make up for some very real gaps in his or her own personality.*

Then each man tied their respective dog's leashes to a tree or a park bench and proceeded to fistfight right there in the park. A policeman who walked up and saw what was happening broke up the fight and gave both men a ticket with a stiff fine. A witness to all the potential mayhem noticed that the two dogs had little or no interest in the fight and sat quietly by, waiting for their owners to finish whatever it was they were doing.

A Pit Bull owner may not like what others say about Pit Bulls in general, or about his or her dog in particular, but overt hostility is not in the best interest of the Pit Bull. In fact, many people want to brand a Pit Bull's owner with the same dangerous tag that they use on the dogs. Maturity is the order of the day. Don't make things worse by acting out when slanderers and verbal abusers confront you because of your dog, especially if that dog is a Pit Bull.

Choosing a Pit Bull

Choosing a Pit Bull takes two tracks:

1. choosing a Pit Bull puppy or
2. choosing an adult Pit Bull.

Some responsible Pit Bull breeders have put a moratorium on breeding and/or selling pet-quality puppies. They have done this due to the glut of adoptable Pit Bulls, of all ages, that are languishing in most animal shelters in the United States. Because adopting a homeless Pit Bull is so important, this book will put more emphasis on this track than on buying a puppy.

Curious and cute, this little Amstaff puppy shows all the charm and appeal that is usually the case in both the American Pit Bull Terrier and the Amstaff.

Pit Bull Puppies

As with many breeds, Pit Bulls as babies are very cute and charming. The best advice that anyone could ever be given regarding any purebred puppy purchase is to study the breed. Come to know the most reputable breeders of that breed. There is one good rule of thumb about how to decide if a breeder is reputable or not: Reputable breeders will want to know as much about you as you want to know about them. Reputable breeders don't sell entire litters and don't do busi-

While young children certainly can supply plenty of love and affection, training a Pit Bull should probably fall to a responsible older child or adult.

the waters of the dog-owning world. Pay attention to what the mentor says, even, and perhaps especially, if the mentor thinks you are all wrong for a Pit Bull.

Adult Pit Bulls, Especially Rescued Pit Bulls

You have several strong allies in finding a good adult Pit Bull. There are many exceptional Pit Bull rescue organizations in every part of the United States. Contact one of these organizations and factually tell them about you and your family. Like reputable breeders, rescue groups will want to know if you are indeed a good candidate to adopt one of their dogs. It is true that there are many more good adoptable Pit Bulls than there are good adoptive homes available. That does not mean that rescue organizations are soft touches. The raw underworld of dogfighters still exists that would like to get their bloody hands on some of the Pit Bulls in shelters and in rescue organizations. Both shelters and rescue groups are very careful to determine that you are who and what you say you are before any serious talk about an adoption takes place.

ness over the telephone or through the Internet. Reputable breeders want to find the best possible homes for any surplus puppies that they may have. It is entirely possible that you may not qualify as a potential puppy purchaser from some reputable breeders. You may not like this but you shouldn't take it too personally; it does speak volumes about the reputation of that Pit Bull breeder.

If you have carefully considered a Pit Bull puppy—and there are sometimes wonderful puppies for adoption at animal shelters or through Pit Bull rescue groups—find yourself a mentor, someone respected within the community of dog breeders. Learn from that mentor and let the mentor help you navigate through

The local animal shelter is also a good place to look for an adoptable adult Pit Bull. Expect the same close scrutiny and thorough background check before you are approved, if you are approved. Both rescue groups and animal shelters have a great deal of experience in assessing the pet characteristics of the Pit Bulls in their care. Due to the background and possible abuse that some dogs have suffered, not

Pit Bull youngsters are cute and adorable, but they grow up. Training a Pit Bull from puppyhood to adulthood requires a real commitment.

all Pit Bulls are good candidates for adoption. Fortunately for you, the shelters and rescue groups have weeded out all but the best potential pets. If a shelter or a rescue group helps you connect with just the right Pit Bull, be generous with your donations to them. They have just put you with a Pit Bull that may well be the best dog you will ever own.

Planning for a Pit Bull

You will need a careful plan of action before you bring either a Pit Bull puppy or an adult Pit Bull into your home. All the points on the *Should I Own a Pit Bull* test should be addressed and resolved long *before* you ever contemplate owning a Pit Bull. If you are lacking in any of those areas, then the Pit Bull is most likely a bad idea for you.

If you have passed the test, continue to go slowly in your efforts to become a Pit Bull owner. Far too many people will get a dog in a hurry and then suffer intensely (as does the dog) for their lack of up-front preparation time. Make the potential obtaining of a Pit Bull a slow, careful, and considerate decision. Look at all the variables in your life. Remember that if you guess wrong and the Pit Bull is not for you, for you it is simply a bad decision, but for the Pit Bull it will probably be a death sentence.

Adopting a Pit Bull

One of the greatest acts of kindness a knowledgeable dog person can do is to adopt an adult Pit Bull. It is true that there may be some hidden issues that have to be ferreted out and resolved, but salvaging a good dog from a fate of almost certain death is, as a small child said, the "goodest of good deeds." Many Pit Bulls have come to an animal shelter or a Humane Society through no fault of their own. Their original owners couldn't have passed the ownership test and the Pit Bull suffered as a result.

More patience is often needed for an adult Pit Bull. Some dogs may have more than one good reason not to expect good treatment from humans. Realistically, some of these dogs, like those that often come to shelters from dogfighters, may need to be euthanized. This would certainly be true of any Pit Bull that showed overt and free-floating aggression toward

Adopting an adult Pit Bull, especially an old smoothy like this one, can be the right choice for many prospective dog owners.

human beings. Still other Pit Bulls might need to be put to sleep if they, because of their breeding or pit history, are hyperaggressive toward all other dogs.

That still leaves a large number of Pit Bulls that aren't specifically aggressive around humans or that show aggressiveness only toward other dogs of the same gender or in threatening situations. This great group of wonderful and definitely reclaimable Pit Bulls are in shelters or fos-

ter care waiting for the right person to come along and give them a home.

Earlier there was a list of many heroic Pit Bulls. These dogs saved their owners' lives or did some other courageous and incredible things. Most of these Pit Bulls were not "pick-of-the-litter" puppies carefully selected for their intelligence and bravery. Most of the heroic Pit Bulls were adopted dogs that had been abused until they reached the right home and the right owner who turned their lives around.

The Real Thrill

There can be few greater thrills for a genuine dog lover than to take a homeless dog off life's refuse pile, add love and care, and then see that dog, like the Phoenix rising from the ashes, become the great dog it was meant to be. Training such a rescued dog may require a little more time, a little more patience, and a little more skill, but the end result is a dog that has been given back its life. A dog owner can ask for no better companion.

A previous chapter mentioned Pit Bulls that were owned by celebrities. Here are some additional celebrities who opened their homes and hearts to rescue Pit Bulls: the versatile actress, Rosie Perez; actor/comedian Sinbad; and actress/singer Bernadette Peters. One of the most vocal celebrities to rescue a Pit Bull is *Exorcist* star Linda Blair. As she recounted on the "O'Reilly Factor" news program, she was followed home one night by a dog, a dog that turned out to be a stray Pit Bull. Rather than being threatened by this dog, Blair gave the dog a home and was introduced to just how good a pet a Pit Bull can be.

Even casual activities like going for a walk with the dog take on added significance when that dog is a Pit Bull capable of exerting a great deal of pulling power.

Taking the Pit Bull Plunge, or Not

Be very sure that you are the right kind of person before you submit a Pit Bull to the agony of not being the right dog for an owner it adores. Carefully weigh all aspects of your life, including the presence of children and other pets, before you take the Pit Bull plunge. If, after taking a careful assessment of yourself and your circumstances, you decide that

a Pit Bull is for you, then best wishes. If you did pass the test and want a Pit Bull, by all means consider adopting one from an animal shelter or from a Pit Bull rescue organization. (Web sites for some rescue groups are in the back of this book.)

If, on the other hand, after careful consideration, you believe that you are not Pit Bull owner material and you opt out of owning a Pit Bull, then congratulations to you! Your realistic self-assessment is both wise and admirable.

5 *Principles of Pit Bull Socialization*

Owning a Pit Bull is a great responsibility and it can be a great joy as well. The responsibility will exist regardless of how you treat or work with your Pit Bull. The joy will come only with proper molding and shaping of the Pit Bull on your part. There is no greater force to bring out the best in a pet than socialization. It can also be said that the poorly socialized Pit Bull, regardless of how much training it may receive, is a potentially unstable animal.

Socialization: Two Targets and One Objective

This chapter will deal with two forms of socialization: socialization of a Pit Bull puppy and socialization of an adult Pit Bull. Puppies are a *tabula rasa,* or blank page upon which a loving, knowledgeable, and careful owner can leave the most positive of imprints. In short, puppies usually grow up to become what you make them.

Rescued adult Pit Bulls are different than impressionable young puppies. They are already past the prime socialization time (6–12 weeks old) of early puppyhood. It is also true that many rescued Pit

Bulls come from a background where negative molding and shaping took place in the form of poor or nonexistent socialization. To further muddy the water for many rescued dogs, there may be no factual history of how the now-adult Pit Bull was raised, what socialization (good or bad) it may have had, or what abuse or maltreatment it may have endured.

In both the socialization of puppies and the socialization of rescued adult Pit Bulls, a patient owner is essential. Puppies need time to develop and a patient and consistent environment is crucial so that development will be positive. Adult Pit Bulls may have some "baggage" from their previous lives that patient and consistent new owners must help them work through before they can be truly acclimatized to their new homes.

Precisely, What Is Socialization?

Socialization is the provision of learning experiences for a canine in order that it have an inventory—or data base, if you prefer—of positive experiences to refer back to when those same or similar experiences are encountered in the future. In

Knowing how to introduce your pet (or yourself) to a strange dog is an important skill that helps the dog not be afraid or aggressive when meeting new humans.

modern parlance, socialization is the programming of your pet's computer with positive data in order that the dog will, after he has retrieved the data in his memory banks, know how to respond.

Knowledgeable pet owners realize that a "no surprises" environment is best. This kind of environment is especially important when the dog involved may be large and powerful—like a Pit Bull. You, as your dog's molder/shaper, want to put your pet in as many situations, with positive outcomes engineered in advance by you, with as many stimuli, and with as many different kinds of people, places, and things as possible. Find the potential variables that your Pit Bull may encounter in its everyday life and then make those first impressions positive.

The Pit Bull's Socialization Journal

It is your job as primary socializer to really think through what you need to include in your dog's socialization *dossier*. Unmarried dog owners or older couples without grandchildren sometimes fail to socialize their dogs to small children. Don't assume that your Pit Bull will like children simply because you do. Put children, fire engines, traffic noise, overhead airplanes, and any possibly frightening or threatening things that may assail your Pit Bull on the list of things with which you want to familiarize your pet.

Providing Socialization for the Pit Bull Puppy

There is thought to be a time-specific window for the most effective socialization for a Pit Bull puppy. Some people believe that any canine can bond with its owner at any age; others point to the age between 6 weeks and 12 weeks of age as the optimal bonding time

Bonding is nothing more than an intense form of socialization where the puppy learns that you are not going to hurt it and that you are going to help meet its basic needs. Bonding takes place at about the same time the mother dog is beginning to give the puppies the cold shoulder of weaning

There is a two-edged sword if you accept the time-specific socialization window. A puppy should probably stay with its mother for seven or eight weeks before coming to its new home. It is also important that your young Pit Bull have

The well-socialized and well-trained Pit Bull is a veritable joy to own and to have as a canine companion.

all its first shots before you start taking it to dog parks and other places where people and pets congregate. To make socialization easier for a young Pit Bull, you must pay attention to the time it needs with its mother, the age it needs to be immunized, and the socialization experience that seems to come easier to a younger Pit Bull.

Pit Bits: *Socializing a Pit Bull puppy is generally easier because no previously bad experiences are there to confuse the puppy. The presence or backlog of negative scenarios in an adult dog's background can be overcome with great care, great patience, and probably professional trainer assistance.*

Ongoing Socialization

Certainly you can continue socializing your Pit Bull throughout its life, but socialization will have its greatest impact, especially with other common animals such as dogs and cats, if that socialization happens early in your puppy's life. It is also crucial that all these socializing experiences are *positive*. Negatives that terrify a puppy within this short season of socialization will probably remain on that dog's list of fearsome things for the rest of its life.

One example involves a young bird dog puppy from an exceptional hunting line. The owner of this puppy took it out into a field for some exercise. The young dog was playfully running and jumping and inadvertently flushed a covey of quail at the same precise moment that it stepped on a briar. The injured puppy ran yelping in pain back to its owner. The youngster that had such great potential never became even an adequate bird dog because it had associated the flying quails with the pain from the briar in its foot.

The reverse of this incident is how farmers used to chicken-proof young

Any and all interactions between dogs in the socialization process must be under controlled and supervised circumstances!

puppies. They would place the puppy in close proximity to a broody hen with chicks or with a cantankerous bantam rooster. After the mother hen or the rooster attacked the puppy, it would never chase or bother chickens again.

That is how socialization works: Through carefully staged introductory events, your Pit Bull puppy will become aware that a person on a bicycle, a person in a wheelchair, a person with a cane or a walker, a toddler, a friendly neighbor, a loud police siren, a crowd of people, a jogger on the street, noisy children, a knock at the door or a doorbell, a person of a different appearance or race from your own, an amiable dog being walked on a leash, the smell of a fire hydrant, and any of a countless number of other things are of no threat to the puppy or you.

Socialization with other, especially older dogs, can take place after a puppy has had all of the first round of its shots.

Home Schooling

Socializing an Adult Pit Bull

Given what you now know about socialization, it is easy to realize that socializing an adopted adult Pit Bull may be somewhat of a challenge. Because you will probably not know exactly what the past history of your pet is, you may want to follow this five-point approach to help socialization, or resocialization, work for an adult Pit Bull:

Socialization for an adult Pit Bull should be on a continual and ongoing basis in and around places with sounds, smells, and other stimuli that may confront the dog.

1. **Be super observant.** Spend as much time as possible with your new adopted Pit Bull. Watch what varying stimuli seem to cause the dog to respond. Perhaps it is a gunshot on TV or a loud argument or a crying child or a slammed door or anything else that seems to bother the Pit Bull.

2. **Keep a "Socialization Diary."** Note both cause and effect. If *certain sounds or other stimuli cause* the dog to crouch or the hair to bristle on its back or any other observable response, make a note of it. Don't theorize about why; just annotate what seemed to be the cause and then what was the observable effect. One person found that carrying a diary was cumbersome while out on walks with her dog so she used a small cassette recorder and softly spoke her observations quietly into it. Ironically, her soft voice aided in helping her dog to relax and get over whatever had caused the negative reaction.

3. **Catalog the seeming causes and the resultant responses.** This is a simple listing of how many times the chirping of a bird (or whatever the outside stimulus was) caused the Pit Bull to prick up its ears and look around, or whatever the response was. Review the list to see how many times this same cause and the same effect scenario occurred. In so doing you have begun to plumb the mind of your adopted adult Pit Bull. Very gradually you are discovering the likes, dislikes, comforts, and fears of your new pet.

4. **Don't skip those things that didn't seem to bother your Pit Bull.** By noticing that things you might have

thought would have got on your dogs nerves didn't, you have connected another piece of the puzzle of what transpired in the life of your Pit Bull before you came along and adopted it.

For example, if the clanging of garbage cans and the sound of the garbage truck in the middle of the night don't cause much agitation in the Pit Bull, you have learned something that may be useful.

5. **Devise ways to transform negative outside influences.** If you have followed the first four steps of this approach, you should have a good inventory of what does and doesn't bother your Pit Bull. If noisy children, for example, cause the dog to be adversely agitated, get some children to walk quietly by while giving your dog soft words—and maybe a treat—as encouragement. Then you can ask the children to walk by making a little more noise and so forth until you have made them a positive, or at least a neutral, influence.

Taking this approach will not only help you learn what makes your dog tick, it will also cause both you and the dog to spend quality time together. Interestingly, as you learn about your Pit Bull, the dog has an opportunity to learn about you. If you yell at the umpire during a televised baseball game, your new pet will gradually learn that baseball makes you only a little crazy and that nothing bad will happen because of these mild outbursts.

Socialization will be a family task. Socialization, like training, simply will not be effective if everybody in the home is not on the same page. If one person allows the dog to become afraid or aggressive or any other negative response when out on a walk, the dog will become even more confused than ever. Everyone in the household needs to understand what socialization is, how socialization works, and how important socialization is to the positive future of this Pit Bull in your family,

The Five-Step Approach could be a good way to have everyone realize they can all have a part in making the Pit Bull into a better member of the family. One person made it like a mystery game with the children striving to uncover more and more of the hidden side of the new dog. Children are often more observant, especially in very subtle areas, than their parents. Let the kids be a part of helping the new adopted family member forget the past. Don't forget to document what you and your family have learned so that you can come up with ways to desensitize the Pit Bull or a plan to keep the dog away from the things that bother it most.

It is not at all uncommon for females of the Pit Bull breeds to adopt puppies of other breeds, as well as other household pets, and to lavish much care and love upon them.

Pit Bits: *A Pit Bull languishing in an animal shelter may be an ideal pet for the right owner. Temperament Testing and passing a Canine Good Citizen Test is both possible and strongly recommended for an adopted adult Pit Bull. Some shelters have already begun temperament assessments for their Pit Bull residents, but expect to have to show the shelter that you are the right kind of owner before you will be allowed to adopt a Pit Bull.*

Natural socialization and training processes always tend to work best. Follow the mother's model in socializing and training her pups.

Possible Pit Bull Socialization Problems

One area that may make socialization efforts much more difficult is the presence of other dogs in the household. If your new rescued Pit Bull has to adapt to two packs, the one that includes the humans and the one that includes the already entrenched other dogs, it may take longer.

Author's Note: This is my opinion and nothing more. I believe a rescued Pit Bull deserves to be an only pet. Other eminently qualified people may agree or disagree with me, but some of the real problems that happen to rescued Pit Bulls happen when there are already other pets in the home.

One of the issues that other pets bring to the socialization process is the constant jockeying for attention and for rungs on the pack hierarchy. Most rescue dogs and especially most rescued Pit Bulls, which often have aggression problems with other dogs of the same gender, deserve to be "only dogs."

There may be some disagreement, but many Pit Bull authorities believe that adult dogs that show any unprovoked aggressiveness toward human beings should be humanely put down. Some also believe that Pit Bulls, such as those that have been bred for generations to fight in dogfights, that are absolutely hyper-aggressive toward all other dogs, should also be put to sleep. This is a controversial point and one that often pits experts against one another. Realistically speaking, no dog that may be or become a

It has been thoroughly documented that even full sibling Pit Bulls that have been raised together may fight under the right circumstances. Always protect your dogs by never leaving them alone together.

danger to human beings or other innocent dogs should be in a position to harm others. The same thing is true about the super-aggressiveness seen in many Pit Bull lines that have been bred, rebred, and inbred for fighting. It does seem reasonable not to blame all dogs of a line, but to take each Pit Bull separately and individually to determine what a proper course of action should be.

Having said that, everyone should remember that the dogs that fall into these two unfortunate categories, the clearly human-aggressive and the irretrievably animal-aggressive make up but a small minority of Pit Bulls. Proper socialization will work with any Pit Bull that doesn't absolutely belong in these two categories. It also is true that no amount of socialization or training can fix the inherited tendencies that these two groups have. To say otherwise is to put ordinary citizens and their pets at great risk.

Sometimes a person with a modicum of experience with other kinds of dogs will preach that Pit Bulls can be trained away from the behavior of aggressiveness. It is possible that a dog not in the two negative categories can be trained to not attack people or animals. To make the statement that *all* Pit Bulls can unequivocally be made safe around other dogs and around humans when the behavior of some dogs on an ongoing basis clearly shows that they cannot is playing with canine fire.

Erring on the Side of Safety

As an author, I choose to err—if I am indeed in error—on the side of safety. What many Pit Bull pundits fail to take into consideration, when they make all-encompassing blanket statements about all Pit Bulls, is the human part of the equation. I have known dog trainers who could train a wolf or hyena to do all manner of tricks. Do I believe that a wolf, a hyena, or

Socialization, especially with older adopted dogs, may require teaching a dog how to play. Some dogs have never known the joy of simply running, jumping, and playing with toys and their owner.

an extremely aggressive Pit Bull is the right pet for everyone? I most certainly do not. What some experts or experienced trainers can do does not translate into what the novice dog owner without years and years of training can do. Most dog books are written for the general public. The general public may or may not follow all of the hints, tips, and suggestions in the dog books that they read. It is simply not safe to tell the average person that he or she can adopt a Pit Bull and have the same kind of success rate that might be found with experienced dog trainers.

Socializing sets the table for the Pit Bull's life with its family. Socializing opens the door for training. Socialization helps prepare a dog for the various sensations and circumstances in which it may find itself. Socialization, especially in the case of adult Pit Bulls from an unknown background, does not constitute an automatic guarantee for behavior or temperament.

Socialization Versus Genetic Heritage

An aspect of socialization that is often underplayed in other kinds of dogs is of great import in the Pit Bull breeds. That aspect is *control*. In order that all the new experiences of socialization be positive ones, control is essential. Control is a watchword for those who want to own a Pit Bull. Control comes in a variety of forms: collars, leashes, kennels, crates, fences, socialization, training (both informal and professional), and by an owner's constant vigilance. When Pit Bulls get in trouble it is always because the control measures broke down somewhere. It is in that one moment when supervision of a dog with young children is lacking that a dog bite occurs; it is in that one instance when the back gate is not firmly latched and a Pit Bull gets out and attacks a neighbor's dog. It is in that fraction of an instant when one's guard is down that something tragic can take place.

Chains

Control is important, yes, but a chain hooked to a tree, or a stake in the ground, or the bumper of a junked Studebaker is

Thorough socialization makes walks and
other outdoor activities not only safer,
but much more fun.

the wrong kind of control. One of the
worst wrongs done to the Pit Bull has
been to keep it on a chain. A chained Pit
Bull, and many other kinds of dogs as
well, is a frustrated Pit Bull. A chained Pit
Bull is an extremely territorial Pit Bull. In
many instances where a child has been
severely injured by a Pit Bull it has been
because the child wanted to walk over
and pet a chained dog. Coming into the
quite literal circle of the dog's turf can be
seen as a threatening move and dogs have
only a few ways to respond to a threat.
One of those is to run away, which the
chain will not let the Pit Bull do. Another
is to cower and roll over on its back, belly
in the air. That is not part of many Pit
Bulls' genetic makeup. That leaves only
one other option left open to a threatened Pit Bull and that is to attack.

Thorough socialization makes walks and
other outdoor activities not only safer,
but much more fun.

Pit Fighter's Concept

The concept of chaining Pit Bulls came
from the dogfighters. They often had a
whole group of Pit Bulls; females for
breeding or fighting, males for breeding
or fighting, extra males and females in
various development phases. Kennel
buildings are expensive and chains and
55-gallon (208-L) drums are cheap. Fighters with 30, 40, or 50 dogs needed only
enough land to chain their dogs out of
reach of each other. The fighters knew
what would happen if they tried to allow
these frenetic, genetic canine battlers to
run freely together. Chaos and a lot of

dead and dying dogs would be the invari-
able result.

These Pit Bulls were an investment to
the dogfighters and allowing slaughter

All dogs deserve a better life than being
chained up. This is even more important to
a very people-oriented canine like the Pit Bull.

This stalwart Pit Bull has an expression that would make trespassers and burglars seek other locales, but most Pit Bulls are too human friendly to be of much use as actual watchdogs.

when there was not financial incentive, such as a wager, was a waste of a valued resource. Chains were a convenient, inexpensive way to control what was perceived as little more than a canine tool. The pit fighters wanted their dogs dangerous to each other. Aggressiveness was an asset to be sought after and to be prized. They had no intentions of bringing each or any, of these dogs into the house to spend an evening as a family pet. The Pit Bull was a means to a grisly end, all that and nothing more.

If nothing else you read or see or hear brings home the callousness of the pit dog fighters, then let the wholesale use of the chain, which became a necessary evil, convince you. While there may have been an occasional pet made out of a fighting line Pit Bull, and while certain dogs had potential as breeders for more of their kind, the average Pit Bull was only a possession.

A State of Perpetual Frustration

Chaining any dog puts that dog in a state of desperate and perpetual anxiety. The dog lives out its existence at the end of a tether. It cannot run across the yard when it spots the master. The chained Pit Bull can't seek shade from the sun or shelter from the elements, other than a drum or barrel put inside the chained circle. If the dog turns over its water bowl, it suffers until some human comes and brings more water. The chain makes the dog angry. It sees other dogs and wants to go to them, but the chain keeps that from happening.

If years of selective breeding hadn't done a number on the Pit Bull, being chained certainly did.

Socialization is all about helping a dog to be comfortable in its environment. Good socialization is a control measure, but it is control coming from a positive human heart. The chain is a control measure, but it comes from the opposite end of the control continuum. Good socialization weaves bonds of control through love. Simply chaining a Pit Bull in the yard, with all the neglect and indifference that such chaining usually implies, is not an act of love. Of course, allowing a Pit Bull to run freely in the neighborhood is even worse.

This Pit Bull is waiting for his turn in a sled dog competition. Without thorough socialization and training, this dog could not participate in this fun and stimulating activity.

6 Probing Pit Bull Aggression

A Primer on Pit Bull Aggression

Pet owners may not want to believe that within their dog lurks many of the same natural instincts that wolves have, but it is true. One of these instinctive behaviors is the aggression response. Aggressive behavior is a perfectly natural outcropping of the natural genetic heritage for survival.

Dogs and wolves do differ in the degree to which they usually respond aggressively. Centuries and centuries of human genetic engineering has somewhat blunted some of the natural impulses of wolves in a majority of domestic breeds

From dogs chosen for hunting, for example, there were developed hounds for trailing, bird dogs for pointing and flushing, greyhounds for coursing after game. Each of these specific behaviors are but truncated versions of the hunting instincts present in wolves. Taking the generalized, raw core of the wolf's genetic makeup, human dog breeders, over thousands of years, remade their canines into an ever-increasing array of first, specialized dog types, and then into specific breeds.

Aggression as a Negative

Throughout the entire history of dog breeding, uncontrolled aggression was viewed negatively. In a pack of hunting hounds, a dog that attacked its packmates was a detriment to the hunt and was usually not tolerated. Aggressive behavior among bird-hunting dogs or retrieving dogs could result in an empty game bag and empty stomachs. At a time when survival often hinged on a successful hunt. negative behaviors could not be allowed.

Well-known pet author and biologist, Dr. Caroline Coile points out that "Breeds of dogs were developed as much for how they behaved as for how they looked." Dogs that attacked other dogs or their human owners were usually disposed of and certainly were rarely chosen to be dams and sires of the next generation of canine companions.

Aggression as a Positive

It would be incorrect to assume that aggressive behavior was always viewed as something to be shunned. Some breeds of

The proper Pit Bull owner will always be alert to situations that could rapidly turn into dogfights.

dogs, among them the American Pit Bull Terrier, the American Staffordshire Terrier, and the Staffordshire Bull Terrier were originally developed and then prized for having a heightened instinct for aggressiveness. As Dr. Coile points out in her article, *Training Secrets for Bully Breeds*: "Just as retrievers retrieve and Greyhounds chase, bully breeds fight."

It is therefore in the dog pit that the ancestors of the APBT, Amstaff, and other "bully" breeds received their genetic heritage of aggressiveness. The pit fighting dogs were bred to use their natural aggressiveness toward other dogs—and sometimes other animals, as well—in harsh, one-on-one battle. It also is safe to say that the dogs that won in the pits survived to reproduce more of their kind.

Two Sides of the Same Coin

The dichotomy of the APBT is further reinforced by Coile who stated: "The genetic heritage [of the Pit Bull] is the same heritage that makes bully breeds so good with people, but so potentially bad with dogs." Therefore, to own an American Pit Bull Terrier, an Amstaff, or one of the related breeds, requires an owner to understand that aggressiveness may take on several forms. Many Pit Bulls, even from families or strains noted for their fighting prowess and heritage, will be animal-aggressive and not human-

aggressive. It is possible that some dogs of all breeds, breed mixtures and types are human aggressive. It is also possible, according to Stratton, that some dogs, even some Pit Bulls, may be aggressive to *both* humans and animals.

Pit Bits: *It is reasonable to assume that Pit Bulls will continue to be animal-aggressive. Such aggression can be controlled, but probably not trained out—contrary to what some Pollyannaish dog trainers believe and put forth. Real experts on the Pit Bull assert that no Pit Bull should ever be expected not to fight with other dogs, EVER! The task then becomes one of keeping the Pit Bull under controlled conditions such as a single-dog household, avoiding letting such dogs run free, by spaying or neutering the Pit Bull, by having a dog-proof fence, and an appropriate leash.*

The rudiments of canine-to-canine aggression and pack behavior are learned in the whelping box with the mother dog serving as a referee.

can occur even within the same litter where one individual evidences more desire to be dominant than its littermates.

While aggressive behavior can vary from individual to individual, from litter to litter, or even from family or strain to family or strain within the American Pit Bull Terrier, the prudent owner must assume that such behavior can occur within any APBT given, as Coile puts it "...the right circumstances." It thus becomes important for anyone who wants to enjoy the companionship of this wonderful breed to lessen the likelihood of these circumstances.

As Dr. Coile points out, animal-aggressive behavior or the fighting instinct in the APBT "...doesn't mean that they are mean. It simply means that, given the right circumstances, they are more likely to follow their innate urge to emerge victorious..."

Differences Among Dogs

As with most other mammals, there are often great differences between different animals within the same heritage. Simply put, not every American Pit Bull Terrier will possess the same drive, the same fiery personality, or the same intensity; some dogs are simply more laid back than others. These differences in temperament

Aggression and Gameness

There is more to the dog pit and to dog-fighting than pure aggression. Most breeds of dogs, and admixtures of breeds, can muster up some aggressive behavior. There is another element in the Pit Bull that made them, according to Richard Stratton, the best pit dogs ever bred. That additional element that brings aggression to its zenith in the Pit Bull is the element of *gameness.*

Some people assume that gameness means viciousness or roughly an equivalent to aggression. That simply is not true. The great, undersized racehorse Seabiscuit could easily be described as *game.* Gameness is simply the ability of a dog to stay the course no matter what. Gameness is the grit that allows a Pit Bull to bite and hold on possibly for hours. It is the dog with the most gameness that outlasts an

Pit Bits: *Aggression is not the same thing as viciousness. Many dogs will show aggression around dogs of the same sex and especially if aggressive signals are being sent from the other dog.*

even more aggressive opponent. Aggression may start the fight, but it is gameness that sees the fight through to the finish.

Therefore, to understand the dog pit, one must mentally visualize dogs that are not only willing to fight, but are willing to fight on and on. Such is the heritage of the Pit Bull, a dog with the aggressiveness to begin a fight and the gameness to finish a fight. Aggression provides the propulsion for the fight while the innate concept of gameness supplies the focus. These two elements, aggression and gameness, are still very much a part of what constitutes the Pit Bull.

The Total Package

To complete the Pit Bull you wrap these two combustible elements, aggressiveness and gameness, in a muscular and athletic package. It has been pointed out that the Pit Bull is not the largest of dogs. Stratton, Colby, and others hold forth that, for its size the Pit Bull may be the strongest of dogs. Remember the "Old Family Red Nose" Pit Bulls? Stratton and others point out, this super family of pit dogs was often among the smallest. Some of the great pit fighters weighed in under 40 pounds (18 kg) in prime fighting condition.

The job of the knowledgeable Pit Bull owner is to harness the instincts of the former pit dogs and provide an environment in which aggression and gameness don't have to be put to the test, intentionally or unintentionally.

The Pit Bull and Dog Aggression

This brief glimpse of the dog pit should be enough to make every Pit Bull owner and potential Pit Bull owner aware of the frightful side of dog aggression. Coile shares an example where two APBT sisters, raised together, lived peacefully for

When a Pit Bull (or any other kind of dog) becomes part of a family pack, it must realize that all the humans are above it in the pack hierarchy.

years until one day some spark set off lingering natural capacities resulting in a bloody fight and ultimately in a new home for one of the sisters.

The only sure way to prevent a dog-aggressive outburst is to prevent the access and the opportunity. If your Pit Bull is always under your control when around other dogs, then aggressive behavior can be stopped before it actually starts. This will mean that you may have to choose to own only one dog. It will mean that you will always have your Pit Bull on a leash when anywhere other than inside your home or with you in your securely fenced backyard. It will also mean that your Pit Bull is always supervised and kept under your watchful eye when even the most remote possibility of a fight is in the offing.

The Adopted Pit Bull

An adopted Pit Bull can still be an excellent choice as a pet and companion. Beginning your journey with an adult Pit Bull is different from starting with a new puppy. For one thing the adults may have already learned behaviors that you may not want. Preventing adult dog aggression becomes a much more immediate issue.

Even if you adopt an adult you can get some idea of its basic temperament from observing how it interacts with other dogs, hopefully under controlled circumstances. Not every Pit Bull is right for every home. If you have a less structured lifestyle, some dogs may not fit in. Some dogs need more structure to help them adapt to a new home.

Preventing Dog-to-Dog Aggression

Assuming for the moment that you own only one dog and that dog is a Pit Bull, preventing fights becomes a matter of limiting opportunity. You carefully pick where you and your Pit Bull go for walks so that you can avoid any places where there are other dogs, especially other free-ranging aggressive dogs.

Your Pit Bull may have bonded with you. This bonding is a two-edged sword. If the two of you are out for a walk and you are confronted by an aggressive dog, your Pit Bull will want to protect you. It is very important that *you* protect your dog by keeping it from getting into a fight. Fighting behavior tends to lead to more fighting behavior. One of the worst mistakes a Pit Bull owner can make is to encourage a fight.

Never allow your pet to "play-fight" with another dog. These play-fights might occur between two dogs separated by a fence. They might occur with two dogs held by strong leashes. Dogfighters call these simulated battles "rolls" and they are a lead-in—sort of like two boys daring each other to knock the chips off each of their shoulders—to real fighting. It is sad to note that there is still a "my dog can whip your dog" mentality in many people, even people who ought to know better.

Play-fighting can quickly escalate into real fighting. One sure way to make a dog more aggressive is to encourage actions that look like aggression. Mock battles are a sure way to make a Pit Bull more fight-oriented. Being fight-oriented is a sure way to make a Pit Bull uncontrollable and a candidate for euthanasia. Don't let your pet learn behaviors that you may never be able to unteach.

If you own another dog or dogs and choose to bring a Pit Bull into your home, make this decision only after careful consideration. (I am already on the record saying this is a bad idea.) If the Pit Bull is a young puppy it will have a better chance to learn its position in the home pack. This may not be so easily done with an adult Pit Bull.

Common Sense and Continual Vigilance

Use some common sense if you do decide to bring in an adult. Remember that even two male Chihuahuas brought into a home setting may behave aggressively toward one another. Two males will generally be more likely to attack each other than a male and a female would. The same thing is true on the distaff side with two females. An ideal pairing would be a spayed female and a neutered male. Stratton and other writers attest to the fact that American Pit Bull Terriers may not be quite as likely to be aggressive toward other dogs of more placid demeanor or that are not Amstaffs, Bull Terriers, Staffordshire Bull Terriers, or any of the bully breeds.

The age of the two dogs to share a household is often a good barometer in avoiding dominance battles. An older dog with a puppy or adolescent is generally a good pairing. A young Pit Bull can learn the rules of the house from an older dog

Pit Bulls have always excelled as farm dogs; but even in a rural setting, good training is a must.

that has already established residency and pack status.

A Pit Bull owner must always be alert to the potential for trouble and have the means to prevent it. I once saw the owner of a superbly trained Pit Bull physically pick up his pet in order to avoid conflict with a yappy, snappy little dog whose owner allowed her dog to run right up to the Pit Bull owner barking and growling menacingly. This was one of the best-trained Pit Bulls that I have ever had the privilege to be around and still the owner/trainer thought he had to step in physically. By lifting his dog off the ground, the owner of the Pit Bull kept a problem from happening, a problem that the small dog's owner didn't even realize she had created.

Learn to Read the Signs

Allowing your Pit Bull to be gradually introduced to strange dogs can be a simple preventive measure. Strong leashes, strong fences, and strong training can help a Pit Bull owner to maintain such a constant state of control, that nonthreatening introductions have time to occur. Pit Bull owners are always the ones that must keep that control. If a fight does occur, the public mentality has already blamed the Pit Bull, regardless of the truth of the matter.

Canine Body Language

Understanding canine body language can help a Pit Bull owner head off trouble before it happens. Most breeds were not bred for fighting, but sometimes dogs of nonbully breeds act like they are real canine warriors. Ironically, Amstaffs, APBTs, and other bully breed dogs are not very dramatic in their reactions to possible aggression. As one APBT owner called it, these dogs take on "...almost an attitude of ominous silence" before they erupt.

Once the Pit Bull breeds reach their boiling point, aggressive behavior seems to come with extreme excitation. This response has been compared to the strike of a rattlesnake. The dog goes from a quiet state and gradually becomes more and more agitated until it erupts in a cascade of violence all over the threatening opponent.

Pit Bulls can show all the classical battle signs. Their eyes lock on the target, up go the ears, the tail goes stiffly out, and the muscles of the body tend to bunch up.

Some dogs, if physically close to the potential opponent, will give the stranger a solid shoulder bump. Often an aggressive dog will try to be *taller* than its adversary. All of these signs signal an impending battle and should sound an alarm for the Pit Bull's owner to take action.

When a Fight Takes Place

Even when two dogs are leashed and being pulled away from each other, some insignificant thing can still trigger a fight. I once saw two APBT owners, each holding on to an excited, aggression-ready dog, lean toward each other to shake hands good-bye when this simple act set both dogs off. Both men knew better, but had failed to note the level of stress being generated in both their dogs,

It is important that a responsible Pit Bull owner try to break the focus of a potentially aggressive dog:

1. Turn your pet so that it cannot see and attempt to *stare down* a potential opponent. This stare is a sure fight sign and also seems to bring out increased hostility in the "staree" and in the "starer."
2. Move immediately away with your pet, turning its line of sight (and stare) away from the other dog.

While some people who don't really know the Pit Bull breeds disagree, you must never allow your Pit Bull to run free and unleashed outside of a securely fenced yard. Never assume that your pet won't somehow catch sight of another dog and rush in harm's way. Never assume that your Pit Bull will not fight. It will, if you let it happen. Mistakes with this breed are of greater magnitude than they are with other breeds. A fast way to add fuel to the public's wrongheadedness about the American Pit Bull Terrier is to relax a moment and let a fight start. Even if neither dog is injured, the Pit Bull cauldron of negative publicity ratchets up a notch or two and boils just a little bit hotter.

Always Remember

Always remember that you own a Pit Bull and that its ancestry can transcend all the training and all other protective measures erected to keep other kinds of dogs out of trouble. Never leave your dog alone and unsupervised with another dog, even if they are friends. Just one moment of neglect can bring great sadness and regret. Remember, in Dr. Coile's account of the two APBT sisters, these dogs were raised together, lived together, and almost died together.

Feeding. There are specific times when dogs need to be separated. One of these is when they are being fed. Fights over food in canines go back even further than the Pit Bull ancestry to the legacy of the wolf. Don't let food become an instigator to a dog fight.

Distractions. Don't become distracted when you have two dogs in close proximity to one another. Like taking your eyes off the road when driving, it takes only a split second of inattention for an accident to occur. Supervise your dogs when they are together. Don't let misbehavior on the part of one dog lead to a battle. Pay attention or separate the dogs.

Be Calm

Fights shouldn't occur if the human is up to the task of preventing them. When they do, don't make things worse by going ballistic. If the fight is between your Pit Bull and another breed, you are more likely to be bitten accidentally by the other dog. If you lose your head you will only make the fight worse. Now is the time to remember the gameness concept. The Pit Bull is probably already locked steadfastly onto the other dog.

The Breaking Stick

You must break that bite hold before you can separate the two dogs. Grabbing one dog or the other won't make your Pit Bull release its hold. For that you will need a *breaking stick*. This piece of wood is a little thicker than a standard ruler. It is so named because when pushed into the gripping dog's mouth just behind the canine teeth, the breaking stick can work as a lever to pry the Pit Bull's mouth open.

When the bite grip is broken, that Pit Bull must be pulled away. If the dogs fighting are both Pit Bulls you are going to need some help with the second Pit Bull.

After you have broken up the battle, separate the dogs to allow hot blood to cool. Once you have seen such a fight and been forced to stop it, you will understand why owning a Pit Bull is such an awesome responsibility. Fortunately, all their redeeming virtues make owning an APBT an awesome privilege.

7 Principles of Pit Bull Training

The Purpose of Training Your Pit Bull

All dogs should be trained and that includes all Pit Bulls. Rescue groups and animal shelters are filled with dogs, all types of dogs, that have had little or no training. Far too many dogs are branded as rambunctious, rowdy, and uncontrollable when it is the owners who have been lazy, negligent, and shortsighted.

Every Dog Deserves Good Training

Any dog deserves the right to be the best pet it can possibly be. That will never happen without human intervention: careful, thought-through, consistent intervention. When humans do not step in with early socialization, basic lessons, and more advanced training, many potentially great dogs are banished to the backyard where they rarely see the humans they adore.

Untrained and unsocialized dogs are seen only rarely, if and when someone thinks to provide dog food and fresh water. During these rare moments, these backyard dogs are overjoyed to see their owners and they react in an understandably joyful and exuberant manner. Confronted with such an excited canine, the neglectful owner believes that putting the dog in the backyard was the right thing to do all along. Thus, because training wasn't a high priority, the subsequent lack of training becomes a self-fulfilling prophecy in that the human part of the equation does not keep the Pit Bull from failing as a good pet.

Training Helps Dogs and Dog Owners Live Happier, Better Lives

For far too many dogs, the backyard is the first station on the road to the humane society or the animal shelter. Once at a shelter, the misunderstood, banished pet becomes a now-abandoned pet. This dog becomes one of many that only want homes with caring and loving humans. Dogs aren't the reason that animal shelters exist; it is human failing that makes it necessary for pets to be placed where adoptions are so often the exception rather than the rule.

If the average dog is thus betrayed by an unthinking and impulsive owner, then how much more is a Pit Bull left with no home and no hope? In this book we have looked at the ways that Pit Bulls can get into trouble and most of these ways have their genesis with a poorly prepared, irresponsible, or inconsiderate owner.

Untrained Pit Bulls Do Not Have a Very Bright Future

Pit Bulls have notoriously been dogs without second chances. That is one of the main reasons that becoming the owner of a Pit Bull should be a decision not entered into lightly and a responsibility not casually undertaken. Impulsive dog owners are almost always bad dog owners. Pit Bulls face an uphill struggle even with the best of owners. A neglected,

Training can take place inside or outside. But it must take place without distractions.

> **Pit Bits:** *Every dog deserves to be trained and this is especially true of a dog like the Pit Bull that may have a certain genetic predisposition of aggressiveness toward other dogs (especially those of the same gender). Training gives a Pit Bull owner an opportunity to reinforce good behavior and correct bad behavior. Without training a Pit Bull, even from a nonhuman heritage is a liability to others, to itself, and to its owner. Training a Pit Bull is essential to owning a Pit Bull!*

unsocialized, and untrained Pit Bull is on a path to certain trouble and probably tragedy.

With the right socialization and training, Pit Bulls are very bright, attentive dogs that can more than fulfill the dreams of even the most hopeful owner. Pit Bulls often do have aggression issues, but the right owner, one that effectively socializes and thoroughly trains his or her dog, will maintain all the appropriate controls to keep trouble and the Pit Bull a wide distance apart.

Pit Bits: *To effectively train your Pit Bull, you should have a well-developed and practical training plan. Everyone in the household must agree with the plan, understand the plan, support the plan, and follow the plan if it is to be successful. Any deviations from the plan by anyone in the home will only cause confusion for the Pit Bull and may even sabotage the plan itself.*

Training Strengthens the Bond Between Pet and Owner

Training your Pit Bull will increase the strength of the bond that should exist between you and your pet. In so doing you will be able to identify and prepare for behavior tendencies and possible problems. Training not only helps the Pit Bull understand what you want it to do, it helps you understand the capacities and capabilities of your dog.

Thorough Training Balances the Mental Side with the Physical Side

The physical power of a Pit Bull must be balanced with a reliable temperament and with strong mental acuity. Training expands a dog's understanding of what its owner wants and how best to comply.

Training evens out the personality of a dog, an aspect that is especially important with a Pit Bull. An untrained dog is left to its own devices as to what it should and should not do. A trained dog comes to learn, from thorough training, that some behaviors are rewarded and some behaviors are not.

A Trained Dog Is Less Stress and More Fun

Training your Pit Bull makes the dog a better companion animal. Imagine what an untrained animal would be like in the close confines of a home or an apartment. Imagine again what the same dog would be like if it were obedient and well mannered.

There are many aspects of the average Pit Bull personality that make these dog absolutely delightful, but many would-be owners never delve that far into their dogs' psyche and personality to really know what they have. In a sense, good training teaches both the dog and the dog owner.

Training Firmly Establishes Who's Who in the Family Pack

If you have children, it is socialization followed by thorough training that establishes the children as upper-level members of the Pit Bull's pack. Many experts agree that many of the bites and dog attacks attributed to Pit Bulls are the direct result of a lack of clearly establishing to the dog

Some training (like house-training) can begin very early in a Pit Bull's life. More involved training must wait for a couple of months to give a puppy a chance to mature enough to learn more complex commands.

and to the children the relative positions of each in the family pack.

Far too many dog owners just assume that a dog will know what it is supposed to know about being a good family pet. Good family pets are made, not born. Training takes the basic instinctual behaviors of a dog and molds and models these instincts into lessons that a dog can easily learn. Even young puppies understand pack behavior, that some members are higher up in the pack than others. By simply taking this instinctual behavior and inserting all the humans in the family at higher spots than the Pit Bull, a potentially major problem is solved.

Having a Trained Pit Bull Is Smart from a Legal Point of View

Much has been written about the mindset of some people against Pit Bulls. If your dog is thoroughly trained, you have already gone a long way toward desensitizing a hostile environment. Be able to demonstrate a well-trained Pit Bull to any naysayers or breed ban proponents in your community. When you do you lessen any liability that might come your way. You may even have also opened some eyes about these dogs. Good training is always the only option open to a person who really cares about owning a Pit Bull.

Practical Approaches to Pit Bull Training

Training a Pit Bull is no harder than training most other dogs. In fact, some Pit Bulls are considerably brighter than some dogs in other breeds and in other broad breed classifications. Unfortunately, because many Pit Bulls have spent their lives chained to some stake in the ground as part of some moron's stable of fighting dogs, many Pit Bulls have not had a chance to show their trainability. By utilizing some

Pit Bulls are very bright and can learn to do anything that any other kind of dog can do. This willing Pit Bull is towing its owner by pulling a wheeled cart.

practical training approaches, the average dog owner can even train the average Pit Bull.

Pack Behavior

There is not a more important concept in dog training, or even in understanding what makes dogs act like they do, than pack behavior. It is interesting that many humans have yet to read about pack behavior when practically every puppy knows it within their first weeks of life. While young Pit Bulls are still crawling around on their bellies in the whelping box, the best dog trainer they will ever know—their mother—is teaching them how life works in the pack system.

The mother dog is not only the source of nourishment and the source of warmth, she is also the undisputed leader of her fledgling pack of Pit pups. From the moment of their birth, this mother has nurtured them. Up to the time that she

Crate training is an essential part of house-training and it also fulfills a key denning behavior instinct that canines have.

weans them, every aspect of their young lives will be monitored by their mother, much in the same way that a mother wolf would care for her cubs in the wild. The average, healthy mother Pit Bull's example as a trainer is clearly defined and is based on teaching techniques human trainers would do well to model and build upon. She trains her puppies:

1. **With fairness.** The mother dog is fair. She treats each puppy from the largest to the smallest with the same level of care. As the puppies grow, the mother metes out punishment when needed in a fair way. She doesn't play favorites in the litter. The human trainer must also train with fairness.
2. **With control.** This female Pit Bull never becomes angry or vicious in enforcing her lessons on her puppies. Her discipline is to correct and educate her puppies, not hurt them. The human trainer must never use physical punishment.
3. **With immediacy.** This mother knows that only those corrections and those rewards done at the time of the act have any value. Puppies have short attention spans and therefore correction must be immediate so that the pups can identify the act with the resulting disciplinary action. The human trainer also must carry out rewards in a timely fashion if the Pit Bull is to understand the consequences of the particular action.
4. **With appropriate action.** Her behavior doesn't injure a puppy for a puppyish misdeed. As with her controlled responses that come without anger, so

This Pit Bull is being taught a hand signal. The dog obeys because it has learned that to do so will mean a reward, often a tasty reward!

are her training efforts appropriate. The human trainer must also always act in an appropriate manner.

Note: One of the biggest mistakes that some novice dog trainers make is to confuse their canine pupil with the wrong word or gesture. For example, if you use the words *"Good boy"* when you are praising the dog for obeying a lesson, don't use *"Good boy"* in an attempt to keep a Pit Bull from showing aggressive behavior toward another dog. *"Good boy"* has come to mean approval, don't use these words (or other common phrases like *"Easy"* or *"OK"*) out of the context in which the dog understands them.

This Pit Bull mother is sharing love and affection with her adorable puppy. In doing so she is showing a model that human dog owners would do well to follow.

5. **With consistency.** The mother dog is consistent in her actions. If noisy barking led to a rough nudge on one occasion, any repeated mistakes of this nature got the same response. The human trainer must be consistent. An act that is disciplined one time cannot be an act that is rewarded or overlooked at another time. Inconsistency really confuses dogs and can ruin an entire training regimen.

6. **With affection.** Maternal love for her puppies is part of her training style. The puppies can sense that their mother loves them and it is this love that makes all the rest of her method work. Affection must be conveyed to a dog in training by a human trainer. Praise and rewards are infinitely more important than discipline and correction.

Following the lessons that are instinctual to a mother Pit Bull is an easy way for a human trainer to build on what a puppy or a dog already knows and understands. When trainers get into trouble trying to teach a dog, it is almost always because they have failed in one of these natural training aspects. We live in a time of new technology and extreme new approaches, but this age of old, maternally inspired training style is still the best. It works because the dog is already experienced with such a training style and it works because it is easy for even a first-time dog trainer to adapt. It also works because it is just good common sense.

Home Schooling

Producing a Pit Bull Training Plan

Now that the mother Pit Bull has provided a road map to training success, it is important to work out a training plan. A training plan is necessary whether you are training a puppy or training (or retraining) an adult. There are several points that a good training plan will include.

■ **There is one primary trainer.** One person in the household (probably an adult) needs to assume the role of dog trainer. Multiple trainers will only serve to confuse the dog and stifle the learning process. Not only do different people tend to emphasize different parts of the basic training, but also their body language and voice inflection may be different. After a dog or puppy has been thoroughly schooled by the principal trainer, other members of the household can be taught how to appropriately use the commands that the Pit Bull has already mastered.

■ **The primary trainer needs to be the "alpha" person in the family pack.** The alpha position harks back to the organization of a wolf pack. In such a pack there is an alpha male, generally the strongest and wisest male that can successfully lead the pack. There is also an alpha female, usually the mate of the alpha male. In a human family, one of the adults (or perhaps a very responsible older teenager) should be the leader as far as the Pit Bull's training is concerned.

■ **The other family/pack members are knowledgeable and supportive of the alpha trainer.** Every other person in a home must be thoroughly aware of what and how the alpha trainer is teaching the Pit Bull. Remember the mother dog's example of consistency? While there will be one primary trainer, there are other humans who will be up the pack ladder from the Pit Bull. All the commands that the puppy or dog learns from the primary trainer must be given in exactly the same way by the other family members. If one person in the group does things differently the entire training effort can be wasted.

■ **A system of negatives and positives (based on rewards for good behavior) must be established.** There should *never* be any corporal or physical punishment given either by the primary trainer or by any of the other family members. A strong *"No!"* is often used, a good way to relay correction to the pet. While some trainers make much of not using this word, they invariably have a word for correction that means the same thing. The word, spoken in a firm, alpha manner, works perfectly well once the Pity Bull has identified *"No!"* with an incorrect action.

There is a strong difference of opinion among trainers and dog people in general about rewarding correct behavior. Some believe that the reward must be some tasty tidbit given after successful completion of a command. Others

This Pit Bull owner is working with her dog with a toy that serves as both a lure and a reward for the pet.

- **Set a precise schedule for training times.** A consistent training time must be established and maintained. By setting up a daily schedule, the Pit Bull, the primary trainer, and the other members of the household can adapt to it. Consistency again plays a part in this period set aside for training.
- **Keep training times short.** Whether the Pit Bull is an adult or a puppy, the training sessions shouldn't last longer than 15 minutes.
- **Training sessions should be conducted away from distractions.** Training sessions should be out of the main flow of traffic in a home. Outside distractions will not help a Pit Bull learn. Other pets and other people should stay out of sight, scent, and sound of the training session.
- **Keeping training sessions focused on training.** It is also important that training times don't disintegrate into play sessions. Training is serious and should be conducted in a firm and businesslike manner and quite separate from playtimes.
- **Each training session should concentrate on one clear, yet reachable, training goal.** There may be many things that a Pit Bull needs to learn, but all of these can't be taught in one session. Keep actual training time centered on the lesson of the day.
- **Be patient with your Pit Bull.** Some dogs learn at a different speed than others. Training should be geared to the Pit Bull's rate of learning. Be patient and consistent and ultimately, the Pit Bull will become proficient at what is being taught.

believe that effusive praise works just as well. Both approaches work, if they are used consistently.

Praise for a Pit Bull has an additional benefit in that it doesn't involve a food item near the dog's mouth. Young children, for example, may have several treats in their hand but they want to give only one. If the dog grabbed more than one treat, a child might be liable to try to take back the treat, which may be a problem. Or what if the child is carrying a candy bar or a hot dog that they don't want the Pit Bull to eat?

The command to *come* is an important lesson that every Pit Bull should know.

■ **Reward immediately.** Going back to the mother dog model, make corrections and give rewards immediately as they are appropriate. Treats given after a training session aren't training rewards; they are snacks.

■ **Always end the training session on a positive note.** Sessions should be concluded with something the Pit Bull has mastered and does well. For example, you may have been trying to teach the Pit Bull *stay.* The dog or puppy is having trouble with this command. After a few minutes of working on the *stay*, stop and end the session with the *sit* command which the dog can readily do. Reward the Pit Bull for the *sit* and stop the training session until another time.

■ **Do an encore performance for the other family members.** When the Pit Bull has really mastered a command, arrange to put the dog or puppy through successful completion of this lesson where the other members of the household can indirectly observe. Do this for *each* of the basic lessons. Not only does this let them see how the Pit Bull is progressing, it also shows them the right way to give the command and the right way to correct or reward the Pit Bull.

■ **Do some role-playing with other members of the household.** After the Pit Bull has been returned to its crate or to another location, go through the actual command with the other household members playing the role of the Pit Bull. Let them understand each component of the lesson as if they were the one being taught it. After going through it with them in the role of the dog or puppy, change places with them

This Staffy Bull has a young owner who has carefully trained her pet using rewards and clicker signals.

Pit Bulls respond well to kind and consistent treatment and to small food treats as rewards for proper obedience to commands.

and let them put you, as the primary trainer, in the Pit Bull's position and correctly give the command and appropriate reward. This is an especially good way to teach children the right way to be supportive of the primary trainer and how to not undo a Pit Bull's learning of a skill.

■ **After the Pit Bull has learned all the basic commands, supervise other family members in giving the commands to the puppy or dog.** Do this with one person at a time and at different times (not all the family at the same time). Help each member to understand why the basic commands are given and why it is important to give the command in the same way each time. If a family member messes up, simply stop the lesson until a later time. Don't be overly critical of the other human beings, either.

■ **(Alternate) Videotape a successful basic training session with the Pit Bull.** There are three reasons that some people have adopted this step: (1) The dog trainer (or any other family members videotaped) can see how the session was conducted and possibly spot ways to improve their training skills; (2) Other family members can review how the primary trainer conducted the session to make certain that they are following this model in their efforts; (3) Ironically, some dog owners are making and keeping a record of their Pit Bull's actual training as a way to fend off anti-Pit Bull forces, insurance companies, or proponents of breed-specific legislation.

8 Pre-Training: A Primer for a Pit Bull Puppy

Begin Early

Pit Bull puppies are adorable, but their training must begin early if it is to be fully successful. While it is unreasonable to assume that an eight-week-old puppy can benefit from sophisticated training, the stage can certainly be set for their later learning. Remember that the mother Pit Bull has already been able to instill some lessons in even her very young puppies. Build on her model of: fairness, control without anger, immediate responsiveness, appropriateness, consistency, and affection.

This chapter is designed for people who have found a reputable Pit Bull breeder—remember that many Pit Bulls of all ages are in animal shelters and they need good homes too—and have decided to obtain a Pit Bull puppy. In my book, *The American Pit Bull Terrier Handbook,* there are a number of ways to help you find the right puppy. We are dealing primarily with training here and with aspects of Pit Bull ownership that impact on training and owning a Pit Bull.

It does bear repeating that the Pit Bull is not the best pet for every individual and for every family. It also is important to restate *that there are thousands upon thousands of adult Pit Bulls up for adoption*. Before you absolutely decide you must buy a puppy, check out what's available at area animal shelters, Pit Bull rescue groups, and Humane Societies. Many excellent dogs and puppies may be available for the right home. You won't know if you don't look for them.

Bringing Your Puppy Home

The First Steps

If at all possible, visit your puppy several times before you actually plan to bring it home; this can be at the breeder or at an animal shelter. By beginning this bonding process, the puppy will become *your* puppy. In order for your puppy to grow into the best-adjusted adult possible, early bonding and socialization is crucial. These early steps are important for any type of dog, but bonding and socialization take on added importance when the adorable puppy will grow to be a dog as potentially strong and powerful as a Pit Bull.

While teaching your Pit Bull to ride in a shopping cart may be taking things to the extreme, it is important to provide as many positive (nonthreatening) experiences with usual objects as possible during the socialization process.

The simple step of visiting the puppy while it is still with the breeder or shelter will mean that your Pit Bull will be going to its new home with friends instead of with strangers. To become the best possible canine companion, this Pit Bull puppy will need to be close to you and share your home throughout its life. Allowing this Pit Bull to live in your home with you and your family does not mean that the youngster will always have free run of your home. Your Pit Bull needs its own specific, special place within your home. This can best be provided by using a cage or crate to serve as your Pit Bull's own home within your home. You can begin to make use of a crate/cage when you take your puppy home for the first time. On the puppy's first automobile ride home, put a couple of old towels in the crate or in case the pup suffers from motion sickness.

Home Schooling

Plant Good Behavior from the Start

Home-training begins the very moment you arrive home, before you actually take the Pit Bull puppy inside your home. What used to be called *house-breaking*, and now is more appropriately referred to as *house-training*, should start right off *before* the new puppy even goes into your home. This home-training begins when you show this impressionable young Pit Bull that the place to void is outside—not inside. Follow these steps to make house-training considerably easier:

■ **Have an already designated outside spot for urination and defecation for your Pit Bull when it has to relieve itself.**

■ **Choose this spot carefully as it will be the normal, everyday, and every night, place you want to train your Pit Bull to use.**

1. For nighttime use and for rainy or cold weather, it should be conveniently near the door you intend to use.
2. For obvious reasons, it should not be in the middle of walkways and places of usual foot traffic.
3. This spot should be close enough to reach when you have a Pit Bull puppy that "really has to go!"

Build on the keen sense of smell that your Pit Bull puppy has. You can encourage this spot as the right place to go by placing some litter there from the puppy's first home that has the scent of its own urine and/or feces.

■ **This first relief time, as you take your Pit Bull puppy from the car, is crucial.** Do this right and you will immeasurably help your puppy to become quickly potty-trained. This is the first training you will give your Pit Bull puppy. Training begins here and now and should occur in this manner:

1. Go from the car to this spot and stay with the puppy as long as it takes until it relieves itself.
2. Enthusiastically praise the puppy for doing the right thing at the right place at the right time.
3. Immediately take the puppy inside to its new home.

Pit Bulls should begin to learn good behavior at a very early age.

4. After the puppy has walked around a little and begun to settle in inside, return the puppy to its crate, which is now in some predetermined location inside your home in a draft-free spot out of direct sunlight.

5. This is not the time to play with the puppy. You are still in the training mode. Your should not confuse a puppy by praising it for doing what it should at the release spot and then going immediately into playtime.

6. Hereafter, every time you come back inside after a relief break, don't automatically go into a play session. By not blurring the line between the reward and positive reinforcement for doing what it is supposed to do at the relief spot and playtime the puppy will not come to associate relieving itself as a precursor for play.

What you have done, in the first few minutes that your Pit Bull has been at your home, is to show the puppy where to go when it has to go. The scent of litter brought from its original home and from its repeated use of this spot will serve as a reminder about what it is to do at this particular place. In microcosm, this is how training your Pit Bull is supposed to work.

You clearly let the puppy know what is expected. If what is expected is what the Pit Bull does, it gets a reward, in this case, praise or possibly a treat. If the puppy does not do what is expected, then it is not praised or given a treat. Rewards are earned and not given simply because you love your Pit Bull. It is not too early to begin teaching that treats come only when certain good behaviors are done.

Remember to stay at the relief spot until the puppy—and this will work with an adult dog as well—either defecates or urinates. You want to be able to reward this Pit Bull for going in the right place. If your Pit Bull does mess up (and that will happen), no nose rubbing in feces or urine, no smacking with a rolled-up newspaper. The puppy doesn't get a reward and the process starts all over again outside, until you can conclude (as you always must) with a positive response.

■ **A second part of house-training comes from not allowing the puppy to go in the wrong place.**

1. You have built your home-training program on the pup or dog's sense of smell. You want that scent to signal to the Pit Bull that it is "OK for me to go here and then I will be rewarded." The smell of urine or feces serves as a natural cue for the Pit Bull to relieve itself. If those smells occur somewhere other than at the special spot, then you, not the Pit Bull, have a problem.

2. Using this natural house-training technique involves not allowing a puppy to get the signal to relieve itself inside. If you see the telltale signs of circling, sniffing the floor, or going toward the door, pick up the young Pit Bull—even if you are too late to stop defecation or urination—and hustle out to the right place.

3. At the spot, you must wait until the Pit Bull either urinates or defecates so that you can end on a positive

note. You must stay out there and can't go in until this happens.

4. To keep little mistakes from becoming bad habits, you must get the scent of urine and feces out of any place where you do not want the puppy to relieve itself. This can be done by utilizing several products sold at pet stores that neutralize the urine and feces smell (one product is *Nature's Miracle* and there are probably others) so that not even a dog's strong nose can pick it up. You must use one of these odor neutralizers, nothing else. Not even shampooing the carpet will work! Some carpet cleaning companies use odor neutralizers for their customers with pets.

Puppy Waste Cleaning Tips

■ It is not enough for you not to be able to smell feces or urine. Dogs have much greater scenting ability than do humans. If the scent is there; they will find it and will believe that this spot with the signal smell is the right place to go, because that is what you have taught it: get the right smell, feces or urine. You certainly don't want your Pit Bull confused about where the right place is to go.

■ You must use the odor neutralizer protects. You cannot mask the smell with Lysol or any in-home cleansers or air fresheners. They won't work.

Author's note: I knew a man who believed that Lysol spray could cover the smell of anything, including puppy urine and feces. He faithfully sprayed every spot where a mistake had occurred and some where no mistake had happened. He found that he had actually trained his young dog to go to the bathroom when it smelled of Lysol spray!

■ If you have had previous pets in your home or you have not been able to stop inevitable mistakes by the Pit Bull puppy you can still use those less than obvious soiled spots by obtaining a "black light," such as those that were used in the old psychedelic days. At night, turn off all lights and pull all the drapes to make a room as dark as possible. Using the "black light," get down near the floor and you will see places where urine and feces have left a trace, then use the odor neutralizer on these hidden spots.

■ Your Pit Bull is bright and will quickly catch on. Remember that until puppies are about six months old, some of them don't have very dependable bladder control. Some trainers report that house-trained puppies will become very anxious and unhappy when they go at the wrong spot.

■ Following this outside/inside program will make the only place around your home where your Pit Bull puppy catches the scent of waste the *right* place!

> **Pit Bits:** *It is essential that everyone in the home understand that your Pit Bull puppy's crate is not a prison. It is also important that the puppy not be returned to the crate as punishment. The crate is the puppy's unique place within your home and, as such it must be a place of comfort and of pleasantness.*

The Puppy's Own Special Place

Your Dog's Den— A Plus and a Must

Your Pit Bull, like all other canines, is a denning creature. Wild canines and dogs of all shapes and sizes have an instinctual preference for a den, lair, or some safe place to which they can go when they are tired, stressed, ill, or simply in need of some quiet time. Most wild canines are born in just such a place. Many domesticated female dogs, left to their own devices, will seek out some dark, quiet, remote place to give birth. A crate for many pet dogs has replaced the den or lair of the wild. Den or crate, the allure for a puppy or dog remains the same—its own special place for rest and relaxation.

Crates, as these man-made dens are generically called, provide a puppy or an adult Pit Bull with a place to go that is its own. This place of refuge or sleep can

double as a mobile container for trips to the veterinarian, to dog shows or similar events, or on vacation. Additionally, the crate is a great aid in helping your Pit Bull feel at home.

How the Crate Aids House-Training

Ironically, the crate, which is substituting for a den in the wild, is an indispensable help in the house-training process. Your Pit Bull's first trainer, the mother dog, has already started your pet's education about the den or the crate. Mother wolves, and dogs that have litters in the wild, are constantly alert for any danger that might harm the cubs or puppies. Canine mothers eat the first stools of their newborn babies, which allows them to recycle the nutrients passed through in their own milk. When the youngsters are old enough to go outside of the den or lair, the mother encourages (by her own example) voiding their wastes away from their sleeping quarters.

The mother does this partially because the accumulated smells of puppy urine and solid wastes make the den a less than pleasant place to be. Another reason is that predators are also drawn by the odors of a den full of cubs or puppies. As the babies grow older, their mother has to often be away from them while she hunts for food. Instinct has made her teach the young dogs to do their business away from the inside of their den.

Size. Even your Pit Bull puppy knows this lesson. Your dog's crate should be big enough for your Pit Bull's projected adult size, but by using partitions to block off much of the inside of the crate, you can make the appropriate size for your puppy. You don't want to leave much more in the crate than turning-around room for a puppy. (Some puppies, even given too much room in their crate, will subdivide and put a bathroom in the back corner. You don't want that to happen.) Instinctively, your little Pit Bull will not want to evacuate waste in its sleeping place. Knowing this fact and using this fact can help you speed up potty training.

Note: Humans who don't know very much about dogs and canine behavior sometimes have misgivings about crates; sometimes crates are incorrectly viewed as little prisons. Nothing could be further from the truth.

Part of house-training any Pit Bull will be the effective and consistent use of a dog's crate that serves as both bed and place when the dog needs to "chill out."

Helping Your Pit Bull Settle In

The Right Way— The First Night in a New Home

Everyone in your family *must* understand the purpose of the crate and its role as a resting place for the puppy. Before your puppy spends its first night in your home you should have already begun the following training segments:

1. You have already begun to teach your puppy the right place to urinate and defecate.

2. Everyone in your household knows that the puppy's relief spot is outside and tries to help the youngster get there in time.

3. No one in your home believes a puppy's nose should be rubbed in any messes it makes.

4. No physical punishment is allowed by any member of the family for any reason—and this is doubly important at the special relief spot!

5. Everyone in the family knows that doors and gates must be shut for the puppy's safety.

You must be sure that everyone knows that the crate is your puppy's regular place for it to be when not being supervised by a responsible person. The puppy has been introduced to the crate in a comforting and nontraumatic manner. For the first time in its life your puppy will now have to adjust to being alone without its mother or littermates.

This first night is very important. In some ways, it is crucial for the rest of the

The crate that you choose for your Pit Bull should be large enough to accommodate him comfortably when he reaches adulthood.

Pit Bull's life. This is a time for the family/pack to be united in doing the right thing for this puppy. *No one that hears the plaintive cries of the young Pit Bull is allowed to take the sad baby Pit Bull out of the crate.* Pampering the Pit Bull now will set the stage for disaster later on for you and this dog. Animal shelters are full of purebred dogs that have never learned to sleep alone in their crates. Much of this lack of learning goes back to some well-meaning but misguided human being who unknowingly has taught the dog that the way to get human attention is to whine and cry in the night.

Now is a time when the entire family must pull together and do what is best for this young Pit Bull. Beginning with the first night in its new home, no matter how sad the puppy sounds or how much someone wants to go to its rescue, the puppy *must* sleep in its crate! Everyone in the family needs to realize that sleeping in its crate is best for the puppy. The youngster, if not messed up by some human being, will soon learn not to cry and that the crate is a place of safety.

Suggestions for Helping the First Night Blues

1. Use an old-fashioned hot water bottle—the rubber kind with no leaks to mess up the puppy's bedroom/den. This will give the pup a sense of warmth somewhat like its mother.
2. Perhaps an item from the puppy's first home that has retained comforting scents could be placed in the carrier to provide it with a little "home" scent.
3. You might use an old wind-up clock (nonelectric, with the alarm deactivated, for sure!) so that its ticking can somewhat simulate the beating of the mother's heart.
4. One modern way to comfort a puppy is to place a radio close by (not in) the crate. Put the radio on low volume and tune it to an all-night talk radio station. This helps the puppy feel that humans are not too far away.

Note: Feed the same food the baby Pit Bull has been eating at its first home. Changing foods now can be traumatic to an inexperienced puppy; you can always

Pit Bits: *Effectively house-training your Pit Bull puppy makes use of instinctive behaviors that are part of what the puppy has already learned from its mother. The puppy should never be punished for relieving itself inside the home. The myths about swatting with a rolled-up newspaper or rubbing a puppy's nose in its own waste are dumb and only make a puppy fear you.*

point. Until this puppy is somewhere between four and six months of age it will have limited bladder control. Don't expect perfection until the puppy matures enough to be able to wait to relieve itself. You certainly don't have to wait six months to begin house-training. You just need to be realistic about what a puppy can and cannot physically do until it matures a bit.

shift to a different diet later. It is also a good idea to feed the puppy on the same schedule it was on at the breeder's or the animal shelter. Regulating when the puppy eats is also a good way to predict when it will have to relieve itself.

House-training a puppy does not need to be the tough job that it has been made out to be. Your little Pit Bull has already begun to bond with you and it doesn't want to displease you. The idea is to let the puppy know *how* to please you. At this early part of your relationship your puppy and you are in complete agreement. Now your part of the house-training task is to help your puppy continue to please you by not making a mess inside.

Canine Instincts and Human Understanding

It doesn't really matter how much your Pit Bull may want to please you at this

Many Pit Bulls have been great K-9 Corps dogs and have returned home to resume their lives as happy family pets.

Crate-Training Suggestions

- Keep a positive attitude about crates and their effective use of instinctual canine behavior in these crates that are serving as a den for your Pit Bull.
- When you buy your first crate buy it large enough for the puppy to use as an adult also. Make a sturdy partition to keep the crate no larger than the puppy actually requires. You can always make the space bigger as the puppy grows.
- Place the crate in an out-of-the-way, but not isolated, place in the home. Be sure that the crate is not in a direct draft or in the sun or the puppy will not be comfortable.
- Put the puppy in the crate for rest periods or when you have to leave the dog unattended for a couple of hours. Upon your return, immediately take the puppy out to the relief spot, praise its activity there, and come right back in.

Important: If you want to go out and play, do so *after* the break is over so the dog will not confuse elimination with exercise or play.

- Use a firm alpha voice to silence any crying or whining when the puppy is placed back into the crate.
- Keep a mat or old towel in the crate along with one your puppy's favorite toys or favorite durable chew toy in the crate to keep the puppy occupied when it isn't sleeping.

- Never feed, water, or give an edible treat to your Pit Bull in its crate. The place for these things is outside the sleeping area.
- Your family and friends will need to understand the continued importance of the crate and how it makes things much better for your Pit Bull.

Do NOT give enthusiastic praise or petting to the puppy for about ten minutes after you let it out of the crate to be with you in the home. Such praise may confuse the puppy and may make it seem that simply getting out of the crate is to be rewarded.

Crate-training takes advantage of the dog's innate desire to keep its den clean, but it does require a regular plan for puppy feeding and then subsequent trips outside. Utilizing crate-training along with a feeding/relief trip schedule, you can greatly simplify house-training. Always remember to reward (and never use a harsh tone or word at the relief spot—the relief spot should be only a place of positive experiences for a puppy—when the puppy does what it is supposed to do where it is supposed to do it.

When to Take the Puppy Out

Some understanding of how a puppy's body works is important. Knowing when your puppy will normally need to relieve itself allows you to establish a regular schedule of going outside. Here are some suggestions about how to time trips outside:

1. Take the puppy out to relieve itself after it eats or drinks. Over a period of time, the additional food or water may cause added pressure to void waste.
2. Take the puppy outside the first thing each morning *immediately after* you take it from the crate.
3. Take the young Pit Bull out after puppy naps during the day.
4. Take the pup out after a long and lively play period.
5. Make a last trip out as late at night as possible.
6. Go out immediately if the little Pit Bull starts signaling that it wants to defecate or urinate, signals such as staying near the door, circling, sniffing, and looking generally ill at ease.

Be realistic—sometimes you will get the puppy outside just in time and sometimes you won't. Don't overreact if the puppy makes a mess. Just go right on outside and stay with the puppy until it *does* relieve itself and has received its reward from you.

When the puppy relieves itself at the right place, consistently reward it, immediately. By doing this consistently, your Pit Bull will come to associate relieving itself with the sights and smells at this particular place and when it does what it needs to do, it gets high praise from you.

What Not to Do

If a puppy defecates or urinates inside, *never* strike it, and, as discussed before, *never* make matters worse by rubbing the puppy's nose in any urine or excrement. Such an illogical action will do absolutely nothing to help the puppy learn, may possibly cause it to fear you, and leave you with a messy puppy to clean up.

By feeding your Pit Bull at regular times you can usually anticipate when the puppy will need to visit outside. If you are using a highly digestible, premium puppy food, the stools should be much firmer with much less volume. This aids colon retention and, if an error is made, the mess isn't as bad to clean up.

Never feed a Pit Bull, puppy or adult, table scraps, even in small amounts. Food designed for humans can upset a dog's system and throw off the balance of a quality food. Feed the puppy about three times a day. Feed adults twice a day. Don't leave food out continuously.

While crate-training is certainly the best form of house-training, it may not work very well for people who can't help the puppy get adjusted to the regular schedule of feeding combined with crate-training. For those people who have to leave the puppy in a laundry room or a bathroom for the adjustment period, a second, perhaps not quite as effective, method for house-training is available. This is called paper-training.

Second Best— Paper-Training

Paper-training involves the confining of a puppy to some easily cleaned room, such as a bathroom, kitchen, or laundry room. It does not work particularly well with outside training because the puppy now has *two* "right" places to go, but paper-

Teaching a Pit Bull to enjoy a bath is accomplished with the aid of a collar and leash.

training may be necessary for those people who cannot constantly stay with the puppy in the first days. Paper-training also works fairly well for the pets of people who live in apartments where getting a puppy outside quickly may not be easily achieved.

Three basic areas are needed within the room established for the puppy's use when you are not with it. A den area, where the puppy's carrier can be placed, a water and food area, and an inside relief spot are all needed within the space allocated for the puppy. The relief spot should be covered with several layers of newspaper or with special puppy pads made for just this purpose. The puppy is

encouraged to relieve itself in this place, on the papers or pads. If observed, the puppy should receive appropriate rewards for going on the papers. Since most dogs don't like to soil their food and water area anymore than they want to mess up their den, the inside relief spot needs to be some distance away from the eating and sleeping places.

By using layers of newspapers or puppy pads, urine and excrement can be removed and disposed of, removing the pad or by simply lifting the top couple of layers of paper. The puppy's scent will remain and this scent, just as it worked outside, will give the puppy an idea of what it is to do here.

Paper-training usually takes a little longer in house-breaking a puppy. Even with paper-training, be sure to walk the puppy early each morning and late each night and after meals when you can. If your schedule prevents you from being with the puppy every time that nature calls, the paper-training method is only a stopgap way of helping your puppy until it has matured more in bladder and colon control.

Neutralize, Neutralize, Neutralize

This bears repeating! If your puppy has an accident somewhere it is not supposed to use, get that area cleaned up as soon as possible. Remember to use an *odor neutralizing* cleaner to get rid of the pup's scent. If a smell lingers, the puppy may logically assume that this place too is an okay site to relieve itself.

If you live in an urban area and your puppy must be walked on city streets and sidewalks *always* pick up and dispose of any excreta. Not only is this a responsible thing to do, it is usually the law!

Preventing Bad Puppy Behaviors

Much has been made of the need for early socialization and early house-training. It is also not too early to stop some potentially negative behaviors before they ever get started. As in so many things about having a Pit Bull puppy, the entire family must be part of the prevention of bad behavior. If everybody in a home but one person follows the rule, that one person will almost certainly cause the Pit Bull to learn some bad habits. Remember, bad habits can be hard to break, but bad behavior can be easily prevented—if everyone understands and complies.

The Dirty Dozen of Bad Pit Bull Behaviors

Bad Pit Bull Behavior #1— Getting Up on a Couch or Bed

Some people may think it is cute to let an adorable puppy sit next to them on a

Pit Bits: *Contrary to what many books and even some trainers may suggest, never play tug-of-war with your Pit Bull puppy. You may be able to win and get the youngster to release whatever you are pulling on while the puppy is still small, but one day as an adult the Pit Bull will win and this will only confuse the dog. Leave tug-of-war out of your Pit Bull's repertoire.*

couch or sleep next to them on a bed. That behavior might seem cute for a tiny Pit Bull puppy, but it won't seem so attractive in a 60-pound adult Pit Bull.

People need to be the only creatures in the home that use couches, chairs, and beds, not the dog. This behavior is easy to prevent, if it is never allowed to start. Only by having a firm rule for the humans in a family to obey can this bad Pit Bull behavior be prevented. *No dogs where dogs are not supposed to be.* As with all

There are several types of collars for special purposes that can be used by Pit Bull owners.

bad habits that a Pit Bull can learn, not allowing them to start trumps having to break the bad habit. Begin by not lifting a Pit Bull puppy up on the couch or bed. A puppy that never begins a bad behavior is not likely to start it in later life.

For an adult dog, placing the dog back on the floor and ignoring it can usually get the point across about staying off couches, chairs, and beds.

Bad Pit Bull Behavior #2— Rushing the Door Each Time It Opens

Some Pit Bulls think that they are supposed to answer the door when the doorbell rings or when someone comes in. This can be a very dangerous behavior for any dog and all the more dangerous if the dog is a Pit Bull. Part of owning a Pit Bull is understanding that control must be absolute and all the time. If your Pit Bull rushes to the door and slips out as someone is coming in, the dog may have any of many things happen to it and most of them are bad. Don't let Pit Bulls start dashing headlong toward a door. Make them wait (in their crates, if necessary) until they are taken outside.

Bad Pit Bull Behavior #3— Playing Tug-of-War

Some people, even some Pit Bull owners, see nothing wrong in a harmless game of tug-of-war. The reality of this behavior is somewhat different. Remember that you, your family, and the Pit Bull are all members of the same pack. Playing tug-of-war with a small puppy is quite different from playing tug-of-war with a powerful adult Pit Bull. Behaviors that may cause one of the pack members (especially a child or a small adult) to compete and lose to a dog are bad behaviors.

It is important to remember that you should want the Pit Bull to not pull something out of your hand or away from you. You can't play this game without the danger of it becoming a bad habit.

Bad Pit Bull Behavior #4— Riding with the Dog's Head Out of the Car Window

One of the biggest mistakes a dog owner can make is to allow a dog to be unrestrained while riding in a car. A dog can be thrown around during an accident or just during a sudden stop or a swerve. Not only can a dog be injured, it can also become a canine missile that could strike the windshield or even the driver. Seat belts for dogs are available and the crate makes a dandy and safe way for a Pit Bull to travel. A second danger of a dog putting its head out of an open window is the possibility of some piece of gravel or other road debris damaging an eye.

A related piece of bad behavior is allowing a Pit Bull to ride unrestrained in the back of a pickup truck. More than one dog owner has arrived home after just such an excursion to find that the Pit Bull saw something more interesting sometime back in the road and jumped out to investigate.

Bad Pit Bull Behavior #5— Playing Roughly with Your Pit Bull

Roughhousing with a Pit Bull is not very smart. Such behavior may trigger a more aggressive approach from a dog, and this is especially true with children. Don't even start playing roughly with a Pit Bull puppy. These dogs don't need to become involved with rough play with the human members of their packs, or with any other humans.

Bad Pit Bull Behavior #6— Encouraging Mock Battles Between Two Dogs

Pit Bulls should never be allowed to play boisterously with other dogs. Only stupid people *sic* their dogs on other dogs, even through a fence or when both dogs are securely attached to leashes. It is far too likely that some innocent bit of play could start a real fight. *Pit Bulls must be kept under control at all times.* Remember, even if another dog starts the trouble, the Pit Bull will *automatically* be blamed for it. Keep your dog out of trouble by keeping it under constant control.

Bad Pit Bull Behavior #7— Pit Bulls Running Free in the Neighborhood

This is bad behavior for any dog and is a death sentence for a Pit Bull. The axiom of always having your Pit Bull under control means that a Pit Bull running free is all wrong. Strong, high fences, sunk into the ground to prevent digging out, sturdy collars and leashes, thorough obedience training, crates and closed gates and doors can help keep a Pit Bull from what might be a fatal jaunt through the neighborhood. Many Pit Bull people don't leave their dogs unsupervised even in their own fenced backyards.

Bad Pit Bull Behavior #8— Adult Pit Bulls Visiting Dog Parks

Dog parks are probably a bad idea for many breeds of dogs, but for an adult Pit Bull they are an invitation to suicide. It might be possible to take a Pit Bull puppy to such a pie-in-the-sky place for socialization with other dogs and with different types of people, but *never* adult Pit Bulls.

Adult Pit Bulls have no business anywhere near such a park. That means that you shouldn't take your adult Pit Bull there even securely restrained by a collar and leash. Dog parks feature the idealistic concept of all our canine friends running free as Nature intended. You might have

This wide array of collars of various types conveys a very important lesson for any Pit Bull owner. Always have a sturdy collar and equally sturdy leash when out for a walk with your dog.

your Pit Bull under control when some one else's dog runs up and starts a fight with your dog. Even if you have all this on videotape and eyewitnesses to verify your pet's innocence, your Pit Bull will still be blamed for the altercation. Protect your pet from the dog park.

Bad Pit Bull Behavior #9— Allowing Unsupervised Children Access to Your Pit Bull

Responsible Pit Bull owners should never allow children and Pit Bulls to interact without alert adult supervision. This is true for children members of the dog's family/pack as well as neighbor children, friends, or relatives. Children don't always realize what their actions may seem like to a dog. If a child gets into a shoving match with a neighbor child and the Pit Bull is standing there, the possibility exists that a simple scuffle could cause the neighbor's child to be bitten, perhaps

severely, by a dog that thought it was protecting a human pack member.

Assume nothing! Pit Bulls can be great with children, but *only* under alert adult supervision. This is also true with Pit Bulls and other dogs and other pets.

Bad Pit Bull Behavior #10— Pit Bulls on a Chain

Dog people have always known that putting a dog on a chain was a bad way to treat a dog. If it is bad for most dogs, it is doubly bad for Pit Bulls. Dogs become quite territorial and quite aggressive if they are tethered to a chain. *Never* allow this to happen to your Pit Bull.

Bad Pit Bull Behavior #11— Having Another Dog in a Pit Bull's Home

This is another of my controversial stances, but your Pit Bull deserves to be

A Pit Bull wearing a prong (or pinch) collar. The collar looks worse than it is, and the dog will only pull against it until it becomes uncomfortable.

The life of a Pit Bull is clearly a behavioral issue, but often it is the behavior of the dog's owner, and not the dog's that can be called into question.

an only pet. Far too many people have thought that two dogs would get along well together, and they do, for maybe a long period of time, and then something happens and a bloody battle takes place. In most instances even dog experts can't figure out exactly what happened to set one or both dogs off. The only way to prevent this is by your Pit Bull being the only dog in the home.

Bad Pit Bull Behavior #12— Your Pit Bull Not Being Spayed or Neutered

There are far too many Pit Bulls in need of homes for you to consider bringing even one more litter into the world. A spayed female Pit Bull and a neutered male Pit Bull will be better companion animals. Spaying or neutering will make your Pit Bull more likely to be more atten-

tive to the humans in its pack. It will also stem a number of hormonal behaviors that, quite frankly, Pit Bulls can't afford to indulge.

Author's Note: If you notice that most of the *Dirty Dozen of Bad Pit Bull Behaviors* are things that dogs can't do anything about, then you are particularly astute. Most of the problems that confront these dogs are human generated or occur because of human negligence.

Your Pit Bull has to be protected from these and other problems that have made life hard for many Pit Bulls, and their owners. You *must* be always alert and watchful for situations that could put your Pit Bull in harm's way. Some breeds of dogs can tolerate casual owners, though not many. The Pit Bull is not one of these. Be strong, assertive, careful, and courageous in protecting your Pit Bull. Think about it—If the roles were reversed, your Pit Bull would do it for you!

9 The Platform of Basic Training

Start Training in a Positive Manner

For a moment, remember your school days and think about how much easier it was to learn something when there was a positive reward in sight. Now compare those positive learning experiences to the times when you have had to learn something based on being punished if you didn't learn it. Of course there are differences between humans and canines, but there are some solid similarities in learning.

Dog training has undergone a radical change in recent years. No longer is the preferred training approach one of simply bending the dog to your will, just to get rote "obedience." Today's best trainers are more concerned in helping develop a dog's mental capacities, problem-solving skills, and intelligence. Hopefully, gone are the intimidating days when brute force made a dog comply with a command.

Modern Trainers: Kinder and Gentler

Modern trainers have developed kinder and gentler training alternatives that are better for the dog and better for the dog owner. Not only does a dog learn more quickly and more easily through positive reinforcement, the dog-human bond doesn't take the beating that was so common in old-style training. Punishment, an aspect that even many older trainers didn't like, has been proven to be not only unnecessary, but extremely ineffective.

By positively reinforcing your Pit Bull when the dog does something right rather than punishing it when it does something wrong, the training process takes on a whole new atmosphere. Your Pit Bull isn't always in the wrong and you aren't always in the role of taskmaster. Your attitude about training becomes much more pleasant and your pet can pick up on your feeling tone.

When you emphasize the positives, your Pit Bull learns to associate specific behaviors with receiving a reward. The reward becomes a learning aid. For example, you give the command to *sit* and when your Pit Bull sits you praise him and give him a tasty treat. With practice and repetition, when your pet hears *"Sit"* he will be more likely to do so because when he does he can expect praise and a treat.

Modern dog trainers have become kinder and gentler, as the old way of forcing a dog to obey has become passé.

The basis of positive reinforcement is having your Pit Bull perform an act for which he is rewarded. Consistently rewarding your dog for performing this act causes the dog to continue to do it. This simple equation is the foundation upon which positive dog training is based.

Keeping Training Positive

Positive training methods can be used even when your Pit Bull is doing something that you don't want him to do. Your dog, for example, is vying for your attention by jumping up on you, which you do not want him to do. To use positive rein-

forcement in this instance, give a command that gets your Pit Bull's attention because he has been rewarded for performing it, as in *"Bullster, sit."*

When Bullster performs the *sit*, which naturally stops him from jumping up on you, praise him and give him his expected reward. Another way to stop inappropriate jumping is to ignore him and give him attention only when he stops jumping up on you. In both methods you have been able to get the behavior from your Pit Bull that you want without having to resort to any disciplinary behavior on your part.

Basic training commands, such as *sit, down,* and *come,* need to be thoroughly taught and positively reinforced. Not only are these commands important in and of themselves, they are also excellent tools to keep Bullster from doing something that you don't want him to do. To make these commands work, the dog must know that praise and a food treat are rewards for performing them.

Another way to eliminate certain inappropriate behaviors is to change the environment. For example, several people are walking their dogs down your street while you and Bullster are in your backyard. Bullster becomes overly excited and begins barking and running up and down the fence line. By removing Bullster from the yard and putting him inside in his crate, the dog is taken away from the cause of his misbehaving. Bullster is not being crated as punishment. Give the dog a break to settle down, cool off, and relax in his crate. Again, you have not had to resort to any disciplinary action in order to cause inappropriate behavior to cease.

Clicker-Training and Positive Reinforcement

Most of us remember the clicker "crickets" that we had as youngsters. The clicker is a matchbox-sized plastic device that has a thin piece of metal that makes a loud, clear "CLICK" when it is flexed by pushing down on it with your thumb. The clicker, when correctly used in dog training, is a sort of auditory promissory note to the dog. Every time a clicker-trained dog hears the click, it knows that it can expect a reward, usually in the form of a food treat and praise. Through the scientific concept of *operant conditioning*, a Pit

Bull trained in this manner will initially be given a treat *each* time a click is heard. The click thus signals to the dog that a treat is forthcoming. Over a period of time food treats for each click are transformed into food treats for a number of clicks.

While clicker-training may not be for everyone—using a clicker does require some specific skills to use correctly and effectively, this method is an excellent way to train a dog. Clicker-training is a fast, effective, and fun way to train.

Clicker-training works in a three-pronged way:

1. A verbal command is given.
2. As the dog is in the process of completing this command a click is sounded.
3. Hearing the click, the dog's correct behavior, in doing the commanded action, is positively reinforced by the expectation of a reward (praise and a treat) when the commanded action is complete.

The key to the clicker is to remember that it comes to mean what the praise words *"Good dog,"* or some other affirmative words, does to a dog. Add to the affirmation the assurance that a treat is forthcoming and you have a much easier and more direct way to train a dog. Clicker-training is not hard to learn and adds a great in-the-process advantage to training in that it allows the clicks that mean rewards while a command is actually being performed.

After a dog has learned that clicks are very positive and that they will result in praise and treats, a dog can be positively reinforced right in the very act of doing

This trainer is teaching her Pit Bull the *down* command.

something good. The clicker helps shape and direct good behaviors and the absence of the clicker can discourage bad behaviors. For example, Bullster is performing the *sit–stay* for a set period of time. As long as he stays in the *sit* he will hear clicks. If he leaves the *sit* position, he will no longer hear the clicks. Instead of an old-time trainer shouting the command over and over again and then having to start the command over and over again, a trainer using the clicker method only has to stop clicking. The clicker is a very precise way to help a dog understand a command and be reinforced in the successful completion of that command. The clicker is also used to release Bullster from a particular ongoing command.

Positive Behaviors Without Negative Pressures

Clicker-training turns a new page in dog training. No longer does a human being have to manhandle a Pit Bull to get that Pit Bull to perform commands. The clicker works because both the *trainer* (the human) and the *trainee* (the dog) are motivated for success. In the now-outdated training styles, rewards were delayed until after the entire commanded act was complete. In clicker-training, the rewards are instantaneous and therefore, positive reinforcement is instantaneous.

Bullster, upon hearing the click, makes a cognitive connection with the sound that the desired behavior is over and the reward (praise and treat) is upcoming. Clicker-training is therefore much more exact. The trainer sees that Bullster is performing correctly and is able to convey to Bullster that fact with a simple click. If Bullster wavers or stops what he is supposed to be doing, the absence of the click is much better than trying to verbally admonish a dog, especially a dog that is some distance away. The reader should know that some trainers don't use clickers for *stays*. If they do, they use a single click as a release signal.

Simply put, Bullster learns that some behaviors are worthy of a reward and that other behaviors are not.

The Clicker as the Sound

There are other forms of dog training that use positive reinforcement as their basis, but clicker-training has become popular because the sound of the clicker is unique. The human voice is not always able to convey the same precision that a single click can to a clicker-trained dog. People talk to, around, and in the presence of their dogs all the time. The click is special in that it is not part of the background noise. The click is startlingly different and is not like the myriad of other sounds that a dog may hear in the course of a day.

Once Bullster has thoroughly made the connection between the click and the prospect of a reward for completing a task, the task becomes important to the dog. The dog actually is learning more than just a specific command; the dog is learning to think. The task becomes a means to the end, an end that the dog wants to achieve.

"Clicker" training is an excellent new approach used to help pet owners train their dogs.

Molding Behavior with the Clicker

This approach to dog training centers on molding and shaping how a dog thinks and therefore how a dog performs. There are two facets to shaping or molding canine behavior:

1. using food treats as an enticement (or lure) to get certain behaviors or
2. waiting until the desired behavior or action occurs on the dog's volition and then rapidly rewarding that behavior or action.

Using treats as lures has as a goal of assisting Bullster in arriving at just the right point that will earn him a click and the subsequent reward. As opposed to waiting for behaviors to happen so that these behaviors can be rewarded, using treats to entice correct actions are quicker. There is another side, however, to using treats to entice behaviors. Experienced dog trainers know that they must "fade" or phase out (to a degree) treat lures so that the dog doesn't come to believe that each and every click deserves a treat. You don't want Bullster's training to be dependent on food treats. Treats should be rewards for good behavior, not the other way around. Lures for training are good in keeping the dog's attention, and in helping direct the dog to the task at hand, but it is important that the attention be on you and on the command.

It is important to remember that in clicker-training, the emphasis must be on the click rather than on the treat. Certainly, the treat is how you teach the dog about the clicker, but the clicker itself must become the training signal for good performance. One way to work away from the *one click–one treat* stage is to start with treats of a certain size and

The *heel* command is the session's lesson for today.

gradually work them down in size. Another, perhaps better approach is to start with a small treat and continue with a small treat. Some animal behaviorists have found that decreasing treat size can, in some cases, adversely affect canine behavioral responses. In any case, never give treats (at any stage) that are large and that can distract the dog from the job of learning how to earn the clicks that bring a treat.

A Note on Treats

Treats don't have to be big to serve their purpose as a reward for specific good performance in training. Too many treats can offset the nutritional balance of a dog's regular diet. If you have ever attended a dog show or seen one on television, you may have noticed that many exhibitors keep some form of treats to cause their dogs to be alert and "showy." A good number of these dog show experts use boiled beef liver or a similar product often cut in cubes or other smaller configurations.

If you watch these exhibitors, they give their show dogs only a very small taste of whatever treat they are using. This is done for several reasons, but the main reason is that a tiny amount of liver or whatever treat they are using will disappear rapidly and leave the dog watching and waiting for more. Training treats should serve a similar purpose. They are small and don't cause a break in the dog's concentration on the lesson at hand.

Some people use dog biscuits as treats. They may do well for some dogs, but other dogs seem to fixate on the crunchiness and have to be reminded of the training. Whatever you use as a lure or as a treat reward should:

1. be small enough to be consumed quickly.
2. be of a consistency that that you can easily handle.
3. be something that the dog likes.

Certain small chunk-size dog foods work well as treats and if they are the dog's regular food, they won't throw off nutritional balance. Liver, as mentioned, seems to work well. Some trainers use foods that are purposely quite different from their dogs' regular diets, such as cheese, small pieces of boned chicken, or

Well-trained Pit Bulls have done very well in temperament testing exercises, far better than some of the breeds usually thought of as popular.

perhaps a bite of one of the commercially available soft treats for dogs.

Praise

Don't neglect the praise portion of the reward Bullster gets for doing well on a command. Just as the clicker is a unique sound and some treats are favorite items not usually in a dog's food dish, praise needs to be more than *"Good dog"* stated in a dull, flat monotone. Some trainers recommend a specific lexicon of praise words used just for training—*"Good sit!"* is an example. Others emphasize words that may have a special meaning for just you and your Pit Bull. A simple *"Good dog"* to mark your satisfaction with the dog's performance is tried and true.

Training Time

Training time should be considered an important part of your daily routine. Training time should always be positive for both you and Bullster. Training time does not have to be lengthy to be effective; in fact, keeping training sessions short and simple actually enhances the learning experience for many dogs. Training should be enjoyable and should never become just another chore. Your Pit Bull is usually very perceptive and can pick up on negative signals that stem from a bad day at

the office or some other of life's hassles. Let this time be special for both of you.

Teaching the Touchies

Some puppies and some adult Pit Bulls may have to be desensitized to being handled. One way to make touching or handling your pet easier is to use a treat. Hold this treat right in front of Bullster with one hand and grasp his collar with the other hand. By praising the dog and allowing him to eat the treat, you can teach him that your lifting his foot or rubbing his ear is a good thing.

Some rescued Pit Bulls may have never received much in the way of positive human touching. Use this treat-and-praise

Pit Bits: *Keep training sessions brief, pleasurable (for you and the puppy), and to the point. Always end on a positive note, even if you have to go back to the last command that the pup thoroughly mastered. Remember, after each training session put the puppy back in its crate for a few minutes to chill out before you or your family begin a playtime. This will help the youngster to learn the difference between playing and learning.*

method to help your pet feel comfortable with your petting and handling him in various ways.

Teaching Attention

You want Bullster to know his name and to give you his attention when he hears his name. Begin teaching his name, as well as gaining his attention, by using a food treat. Hold the treat in your left hand about waist high. Repeat the dog's name and some word you want to use such as *"Here"* to draw his attention to both you and the treat.

When Bullster looks directly at you, if you are using the clicker method, click or say *"Yes"* or *"Right"* or whatever praise word you want to use for positive reinforcement. Right after the praise word or the click, give Bullster the treat, using your right hand. If Bullster doesn't give you his full attention, don't reward him. Using this method, you can gradually

keep Bullster's attention for increasingly longer periods of time. Effective training occurs when you and your Pit Bull are attentive to each other.

Teaching the Collar and Leash

Your Pit Bull, whether it is an adult or a puppy, will need to be comfortable with a collar and a leash. Your regular training leash should be about 6 feet long (1.8 m) and be half an inch to an inch (1.25 to 2.5 cm) in width. It can be made of several materials: leather, nylon, or cotton webbing. It is important that the leash is comfortable for you and of an appropriate length for your Pit Bull. Because some Pit Bulls are larger than others, let the dog's size dictate the precise length of leash you will need for training and for going on walks. You will want a leash with enough strength to help you get your Pit Bull under control or out of a bad spot, if necessary. You will also want a leash that can be useful in keeping Bullster close to you in training.

Bullster's collar can also be made of leather, nylon, or cotton webbing. Some experts are now suggesting the head collars that work both gently and firmly to control your Pit Bull. Head collars—*HALTI* is one brand name; *Gentle Leader* is another—are less harsh than the prong collars and choke collars. Head collars give good control by causing Bullster's head to turn each time he pulls or lunges on the leash. This eliminates your having to get into a tug-of-war to control your Pit Bull. You have control when you need it and you don't have to use brute force to gain that control. These head collars mesh well with the concept of positive training. Make sure the collar fits; an ill-fitting collar is uncomfortable and dangerous. A dog that can slip out of the collar could run out into the street or get into trouble in many ways. Always try the collar on and see that you can put two fingers under it when the it is buckled.

Introducing your Pit Bull to his collar shouldn't be a traumatic experience. For a Pit Bull puppy try introducing the collar right before mealtime or naptime. By having a meal or a nap as an expected event, the collar becomes an afterthought that soon becomes easily accepted.

Let Bullster walk around, in his home or fenced backyard, with his collar and leash on in brief time spans. By gradually introducing the collar and the leash in his home or his backyard, Bullster isn't afraid or irritated when you start using them for walks and training.

Basic Training for Your Pit Bull

There are five commands that many dog trainers consider elemental in what your Pit Bull needs to know and that serve as the foundation for most other training. The commands listed here work well with the positive reinforcement form of training that helps your Pit Bull learn in a gentle and fun way. Take your time and teach your Pit Bull these basic training commands. For the most part they are not difficult for either a puppy or for an adult

Training the *sit* command.

rescued dog that may not have been given much in the way of training. Different trainers may have a different order in which to teach these basic commands, but the *sit* seems to be easy to teach and can also serve as a good launching pad for the other commands.

Sit

The *sit* is a very useful command. It can do more than just have Bullster or Bullette to sit politely on your command—or when you click and command. A dog in the *sit* is under control. For example, when Bullster is sitting, he isn't jumping up on you or nosing around in the cat's litter box.

Frankly, the *sit* is a useful command that, when thoroughly learned, can serve as a good way to put an unruly Pit Bull under control.

1. Start the *sit* with a treat that your Pit Bull likes.
2. Call the dog by name to make sure that you and the treat have Bullster's attention.
3. When Bullster comes up to you, all ready for a treat, keep the treat only an inch or so over his head; if you hold it too high, Bullster may want to rear up on his back legs.
4. Keep the treat in motion, slowly going back over his head. His nose will follow the treat and this will force his head back.
5. When Bullster's head is going up and back, there is a great tendency for him to sit. When he does sit, give him a praise word *"Yes"* or *"Good"* (or click), and give him the treat.

The next time that you try this, or several times to get it right, when Bullster starts to go into a sitting motion give the verbal command *"Sit."* You can then reward Bullster as you did the first time. Especially if you are using a clicker, you can reinforce Bullster as he begins to sit. After you have done the *sit* with the praise word or click and a treat reward, you can gradually, as was discussed in using a clicker to train, phase out a treat each time the *sit* command is given.

By using the *sit* command at times when your Pit Bull is excited, such as at feeding times, when you are about to go for a walk, or when you have guests in your home, this command becomes a good way to support and reinforce good behavior. Always preface this command with your Pit Bull's name as in, *"Bullster, sit."* You not only gain his attention, but you get an effective way to move into other activities that require your dog's attention in a controlled state. Always remember your praise word (or click) to reinforce to Bullster that a treat reward will be earned by performing this command. And don't forget the praise.

Stand

Once the *sit* is firmly in Bullster's repertoire, you can use this *here-comes-a-treat* approach to teach other commands.

1. From the *sit*, hold the treat in a similar way as you did in teaching the *sit*.
2. When you have his attention and he is watching the treat, instead of moving the treat back over his head, bring it straight toward you and away from him.
3. Bullster, intent on the treat, will have to stand up in order to follow the treat. When he does, tell him to *stand* and use the click or praise word when he does and give him the treat.

As with teaching the *sit*, the *stand* is easily learned by using this here-comes-a-treat method. While he was in a *sit*, you have gotten Bullster's attention and you have used his name followed by the *stand* command, with your click or praise word to reinforce the fact that getting to his feet is the right thing to do when he hears this command. As with the *sit*, repeat the *stand* several times for him to get the idea. Always give a praise reward and, as with the *sit*, you can gradually cease giving a treat with each *stand*, after he is doing it well.

The *stand* is important for you to teach your Pit Bull. It is standard operating procedure with show dogs that must be in a *stand* so that the judge can go over the dog. It is also a good command for the time when you are going to bathe and groom your Pit Bull.

Down

The *down* is also done by starting in the *sit* and using the *here-comes-a-treat* approach.

1. With the treat out in front of Bullster's nose, slowly move the treat down toward the floor (or ground) and just a bit forward from where the dog is.
2. Bullster will follow the treat downward and slightly outward. (You don't want to focus the treat right down between Bullster's front legs but a little to the front of them.) The object is to get Bullster's chest to go all the way down. You want to have the treat to be right about where Bullster's nose is when his is in the *down*.
3. As with the *sit* and the *stand*, just as Bullster reaches the proper *down* position you will want to say *"Down,"* using your clicker or praise word as reinforcement as Bullster is moving in the right direction.
4. You then reward the dog with the treat and with praise for having done the *down*.
5. Repeat the *down* as you have the other commands. You will be able to

Training the *down* command.

gradually phase out a treat each and every time you give the *down* command, but be sure that Bullster is performing the *down* correctly and earning his treat for doing so until you make the modification.

Stay

Bullster should have mastered the *sit*, the *stand*, and the *down* before you begin teaching the *stay*. The *stay* is a little more complex and takes some dogs a little longer to learn. In the *sit*, the *stand*, and the *down* Bullster is given a command to do a specific movement. When he does this specific movement he is rewarded. With the *stay* you want Bullster to *not* do a specific movement and to remain in whatever his last position was.

101

Since Bullster knows the first three "movement commands" well, combine these commands with the *stay*. Essentially, then, you are teaching Bullster to *sit–stay*, *stand–stay*, and *down–stay*

1. Start with the old reliable *sit*.
2. Once Bullster is sitting, delay giving the treat or praise, keeping Bullster sitting there. Give the *stay* command.
3. Bullster may take a little time grasping that there is more to what you have asked him to do than simply *sit*. Even if he stays sitting there for just a few seconds after you have said *"Stay,"* reward and praise him. Bullster may not have stayed more than just a moment, but he stayed! Remember that the clicker serves as a release cue.

With patience you can extend the length of the stay as Bullster catches on to what you want beyond the *sit*, *stand*, or *down*.

Another element must be added to the stay: the release word. You can use *"OK"* or *"All right,"* or some similar word prior to praise and reward to let Bullster know that the *stay* part of his job is now complete: *"OK, good boy!"*

There may be some very short stays when you first start teaching this command. Bullster may stop the *sit–stay* before you want him to. Start back with the *sit* and add *stay*. Even if the *stay* is for just a few seconds, give him the release word and reward him. Remember, you want to ignore bad behavior and reward good behavior. Clicks or praise words can help Bullster know he is doing well by not moving. Sooner or later he will grasp that simply by remaining in a *sit*, a *stand*, or a

down he will earn a reward (a click or praise word) and a treat.

Yet another component is involved in the *stay*—proximity or nearness to you.

1. Bullster may be right at your feet when he is first learning the command, but in very small increments, begin moving away from him while he is in a *stay*.
2. Ever so gradually move away from Bullster as you are increasing the length of his *stays*.
3. Start with the *sit–stay* and begin again with the *stand*, even if you want a *stand–stay*, which not all trainers use, and then a *down–stay*. Start each combination *stay* as if it was for the first time.

Bullster should, with patience and consistent repetitions, soon be able to attain half a minute *stays* and then minute *stays*. Be kind to your dog; don't expect extremely long *stays* when you are just starting out. Each dog (and each age) seems to have a plateau where he or she peaks in a particular command. Try to determine what your Pit Bull's peak is and be satisfied with that level of performance. That does not mean that you should ever be satisfied with mediocre performance; just fit the training and the reinforcement to the dog.

Come

The average person may not believe that teaching a dog to *come* is very difficult. Actually, the *come* (or *recall*) isn't hard for a dog to learn, but it is a command that deserves some attention on your part. The fact that Bullster will come to you without being called really means nothing. He may sit, stand, or lie down without being told to, but that really isn't the object of dog training; you want Bullster to do these things when he is told to do so.

There is a big difference between Bullster coming to you because he wants to and coming to you because he has heard his name followed by the command *"Come."* Casually coming to you of his own volition should never involve an earned reward. The command *"Come"* should signal to Bullster that he should come to you—clickers and praise words can provide some speed and directional help—and for that he can expect praise and a treat.

As with the *sit*, try to gauge when Bullster is just beginning to come to you. Make it a real command by saying, *"Bullster, come!"* When he arrives give him a treat and praise. If after you say, *"Bullster, come,"* he doesn't come, you must go to where he is. Let him see the treat in your hand and start the process over again. The treat and his name should serve to get and hold his attention.

Call Bullster a number of times, but don't be satisfied if he runs up for a treat and dashes away again. You want your Pit Bull to come to you and arrive there in control. When he comes to you, put him in a *sit* before you give him a treat and praise reward. You also don't want to call your Pit Bull to you and have her jumping all over you trying to get at the treat. The object of the *come* is to have your pet come to you and be ready for your next command, not just to come to you to get a treat.

Training the *come* command.

Many dog owners mess up the *come.* They actually can make their dog *not* come to them. It is important to never let your dog associate the word *"Come"* with something bad. If that association is made, your pet would be truly stupid to come to you when you use that term. If you have to take your dog to the veterinarian, give the dog a bath, or stop playtime or anything that could be seen as a negative, you must go to the dog to take him where you want. Don't ruin the *come* command—and don't allow anyone in you household to ruin the *come* command—by inappropriate misuse.

Training Tip

Never stop training your pet. Continually run through these basic commands, even if your Pit Bull has mastered them and moved on to bigger and better things. The basics are commands that can be used

If you're not able to train your Pit Bull, you should take him to a qualified professional.

in many dog–human activities. They are also excellent in transforming your Pit Bull from an undisciplined, unruly animal into a companion that is disciplined and fun to be around.

Take full advantage of the gentle and highly effective positive reinforcement approach to training. Some of us were taught the old ways many decades ago and have had to relearn the modern methods. Positive reinforcement makes training much easier and simpler and a whole lot more fun! Well, you know what they always say: you *can* teach an old dog trainer new tricks!

Picking a Training School

There is no excuse today for the dog owner who woefully bleats, "I can't seem

to train my dog." This human whimpering is an excuse for either laziness or cowardice, or both. Every dog deserves to be trained, especially a dog of the Pit Bull breeds. If the person who so wanted the dog can't spend the time and effort to train it, perhaps getting the dog was a mistake to begin with.

So, for some reason you can't seem to teach your pet the five simple starter commands, you can't throw in the towel just like that. If you can't, or more likely won't, train your dog there are scads and scads of excellent training schools, puppy kindergartens, and obedience classes. You can find them in your local phone book or if that fails, contact some of the Web sites supplied in the back of this book,

Finding a good training class is relatively easy. Most of them are good or they would have gone out of business. Here are some ways to find a resource for training and to evaluate it when you find it:

- Try the Association of Pet Dog Trainers (APDT) or the National Association of Dog Obedience Instructors (NADOI). Somewhere in these organizations you should be able to find a training group to help you.
- Contact a local obedience club or all-breed dog club. For American Staffordshire Terriers, Staffordshire Bull Terriers, and Bull Terriers you can find obedience clubs in each state on the American Kennel Club Web site.
- Start where you got your Pit Bull: the reputable breeder, the animal shelter, or the rescue group. These sources all want the best for your pet and should have feelers out in the dog-training community.

■ Talk with your veterinarian. Many pet doctors are well aware of the training classes in their communities.

■ Contact a breed club—APBT, Amstaff, Staffybull, Bull Terrier. Many breed clubs know trainers they have faith in and can recommend.

■ Contact the big all-breed registries: the AKC, the UKC, and the ADBA. Many of these national organizations have regional reps or others that can help you find a local training class.

■ Contact other owners (reputable owners) of the Pit Bull breeds. Some of them will know where you can get a line on a training group.

Things to Watch for in a Training Organization

Dog training classes are like any other enterprise; there are the really good organizations and there are the not-so-good ones. Follow these hints to tell the difference:

1. What is your first impression of the place? Are these people well organized? Do the people there look professional? Is the place clean? If you don't feel right about the place, you are probably right about the place!

2. Do the people there seem more interested in your pet or your check? Certainly, organizations need to make money, but does that motivation seem to be their primary goal?

3. Did they blink when you mentioned you wanted to enroll a Pit Bull?

Surprisingly, there are some trainers who have fallen prey to the myth and the hype and don't like Pit Bulls.

4. What about the feeling tone of the people there? Are they genuinely interested in helping you and your pet to get trained?

5. What style training to they do or do they advocate? There are some organizations that are really tough on the dogs or the dog owners, or both! Ask what their emphasis in training is. Is correction another word for punishment?

6. From your exposure to training, is their focus amenable to yours? Do they even offer the kind of training that you want or is their approach something that "only they know how to use"?

7. Is enrolling in their class the beginning of a self-help or pyramid scheme. On my pet-talk radio show several years ago, I invited a dog trainer to be a guest and regretted it when I discovered that this person not only trained dogs but could supply all kinds of supplements, herbal cures, hex removers, and other items. You want to train your Pit Bull, not become an independent entrepreneur.

8. Does the "Big Name Dog Trainer," whose name is on the front door, actually come to the classes or are they run by student trainers?

9. Finally, you can tell a great deal about how good a training organization is by what they require of *you*. A training class that sincerely has your pet's well-being as a prime concern will want to be sure that you will not be harsh with your Pit Bull or that you won't drop out mid-way through the class with

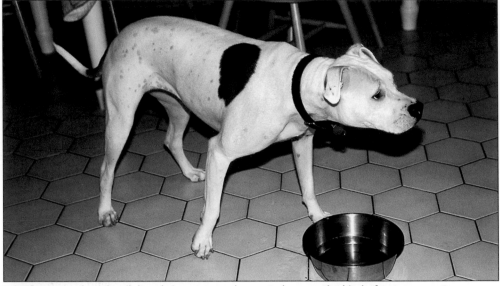

Whether you adopt an adult or bring a puppy home, to become the kind of pet you want, the Pit Bull should live inside with you as part of your family.

only a half-trained dog as a result. (Remember how hard it should have been to get a Pit Bull from a reputable breeder, an animal shelter, or a rescue group? You want to see that same dedication from the training group.)

Using a Professional Dog Trainer

There are occasions when you have no choice but to hire a professional trainer to help you. If you have a first-rate professional in your area and you have an adopted rescue Pit Bull, you may be wise to factor in the expense of this trainer.

You can find trainers in much the same way that you can find training classes. You should also hold them to the same criteria that apply to evaluating training classes. Trainers do offer a real advantage in that they can isolate on and with you on your Pit Bull. Private classes from a trainer are more expensive, but results are usually gained faster and with a greater degree of certainty.

Trainers have a variety of styles. Some of these approaches may be very alien to you, but judge them by their results. Before you enter into any kind of an agreement, ask for people in your neighborhood or locale, especially Pit Bull people, who have used this trainer's services. Call them—and make sure you aren't talking to the trainer's brother-in-law—and ask them for their opinion of the trainer and the methods used.

Restraints

Prong Collars

Prong collars are heavier-duty than the traditional training collar. These collars are made up of a dozen or so hinged, dull, wire prongs. When the dog is standing still, the collar is hanging benignly around his neck like a loose necklace. When the collar is attached to the leash and the dog starts to pull, the prongs press against the neck and cause an amount of discomfort depending on the amount of pulling forward the dog is doing.

I have seen huge dogs with a real passion for dragging their tiny owners up and down the street stop pulling immediately when the prong collar pinches their neck. I don't usually recommend these collars, except when being able to safely walk the Pit Bull (only an adult Pit Bull) would be impossible. For the small person with the strong dog, sad to say, these collars are an option.

Head Halters

A similar and less barbaric-appearing antipull device is called the head halter. Not long on the market, these cleverly designed devices might look restrictive to the dog, but really don't hurt. They function with a strap that crosses over the dog's muzzle and then loops behind the dog's head. The leash is attached to the head halter with a D-ring that is under the dog's chin.

Patterned somewhat like bozals, hackamores, and halters for horses, the head halter works on the principle that the head leads and the body will follow. Head halters look like muzzles, but they are less dramatic in effect than are prong collars and they work just about as well.

Muzzles

Muzzles keep a dog from being able to bite. They are used by animal control officers, veterinarians, dog groomers, and some pet owners. Sadly, there are muzzle laws facing the Pit Bull breeds in some locales. I have always been of two minds about muzzles. On one hand, I like the idea that a biter is unable to bite. On the other hand, a Pit Bull being forced to wear a muzzle simply because he is a Pit Bull rankles my sense of justice. I have always thought that a muzzle was a tacit admission that "Yes, this dog will bite you, if it can." That is simply not the case for many of the Pit Bull breeds. Many trainers believe that all dogs, regardless of size or breed type, should learn to wear a muzzle.

There is the "Caesar's wife" approach that being a Pit Bull means that the dog is going to be held to a higher standard, and a muzzle just reflects your agreeing with that standard. I suppose that a spayed or neutered muzzled Pit Bull that is allowed to spend its days with its owner is better than a Pit Bull that is confiscated from its owner by a breed ban law. Muzzles, under most circumstances, are a last resort, unless they are to be applied to knee-jerk politicians and sensation-seeking journalists.

One lesson not only for the American Pit Bull Terrier and the Amstaff but for most of the other terrier breeds is to provide a lot of physical activity that results in a tired and healthy youngster at the end of a busy day.

10 The Well-Trained Adult (Rescued) Pit Bull

Providing a Home for a Rescued Pit Bull

Pit Bulls have become the single most likely dog type to be available for adoption in many parts of the United States. Poorly prepared owners, not fully socialized Pit Bulls, and bans stemming from breed-specific legislation have flooded many animal shelters with purebred and mixed Pit Bulls.

Candidly, some Pit Bulls in shelters have real problems. Some of them are quite aggressive toward other animals in general and unfortunately, in some Pit Bulls, human aggression is the reason for their being surrendered to a shelter. Other Pit Bulls have had their good temperaments twisted and bent by abusive or neglectful homes. Some of these Pit Bulls can be revitalized in the hands of an experienced and caring new owner. For others no amount of work will transform them into a safe pet with a predictable temperament.

Proving of a Pit Bull: Tough Choices

Shelters and rescue groups that follow guidelines like those established by the Animal Farm Foundation have some tough decisions to make regarding some Pit Bulls. These are life-and-death decisions made by people who sincerely care about Pit Bulls and have to make the tough calls largely because of poor breeders or impulsive owners. Pit Bulls that show any unprovoked aggression toward human beings are humanely euthanized,

Pit Bits: *Many rescued Pit Bulls become excellent pets for the right owners. It seems that dogs that have not had the right kind of homes and human companionship really warm up to good homes with good people.*

Bad behavior in Pit Bulls, as in other dog breeds, is the result of both genetic inheritance and environmental influence.

as are Pit Bulls that are uncontrollably aggressive toward all other dogs. A third group, those Pit Bulls that show aggression toward only dogs of the same gender or under certain determinate conditions are usually given an opportunity to be rehomed.

The Presence of Preexisting Problems

Adult dogs of all breeds have temperaments that are a delicate balance between the *nature–nurture* continuum. Essentially, dogs are the products of both their genetic heritages and the environmental influences in their lives. Both of these forces are at work in Pit Bulls. In

some dogs their natural genetic makeup is more powerful and determines how the dog will act and react. In other dogs, things that have happened to them hold sway over their genetic composition.

Types of Abuse

It is not to be automatically assumed that every adult Pit Bull that needs a home has been the victim of abuse of any kind. In some cases, and perhaps in many cases, rescued Pit Bulls had been in homes where they were loved and given excellent care. Unavoidable circumstances such as divorce or an owner's illness or death may have forced the need for a new home for a well-adjusted pet. Having said that, there are also homes where abuse was present and the Pit Bulls from these homes are rescued in every sense of that word.

Direct abuse is obvious. This involves clearly cruel, insidious acts of violence toward a dog. Hitting, kicking, and other kinds of physical maltreatment are quite obviously abusive. Indirect abuse is something more subtle and more hidden. Indirect abuse, as it is with abused children, may actually be more traumatizing to a dog over the long run than temporary tirades of direct physical abuse. Indirect abuse hinges on neglect, indifference, and complacency.

Many dog owners who would never think of striking their dog will forget to see that the water bowl is full, that food is given on a daily basis, and that attention is given to even the most basic needs of the "beloved family pet." It is the indirect abuser who is content to chain a Pit Bull and let the dog languish, away from human care, human concern, and human contact. For all the regard for Pit Bulls that the dogfighting fraternity says they have, their overwhelming, almost institutionalized indirect abuse makes liars of them all.

It is this indirect abuse that many adoptive Pit Bull owners must undo. Dogs left ignored and neglected have never had an opportunity to truly bond with a human being. The bonding that must take place before rehoming can truly be successful. All the elements of pack behavior and training discussed in Chapter 8 can be overlaid on the adult dog, but only after the bonding process has been established.

The Bonding Process

Bonding with an adult Pit Bull may be easier than you think. A dog that has never really known a caring owner may respond quite favorably to someone who really wants a hands-on, loving pet. There are some points to remember about the bonding process:

- **Information.** You need all the information and observations about the adult Pit Bull that you can get. Knowing what frightens a dog or what the Pit Bull seems to enjoy can help you avoid the bad and accentuate the good.
- **Expectations.** The bonding process is different with different Pit Bulls. Some dogs may bond very quickly and other Pit Bulls may take some time. Don't become discouraged if your Pit Bull doesn't fall in love with you overnight.

Pit Bits: *Try to find out all you can about the background and history of an adult Pit Bull before you commit to adoption. Some dogs have been so negatively used and abused that rehoming them may be well beyond the experience or capacity of some people.*

- **Setting.** You cannot successfully bond with a Pit Bull in the middle of a carnival atmosphere. The dog needs to get to know you and you need to get to know the dog. That won't happen in a chaotic environment.
- **Consistency.** Just as training requires a sameness of approach, so does bonding with an adult Pit Bull. If you are manic one day and depressive the next, your Pit Bull may not figure out just who you really are.
- **Patience.** Bonding with you may have to overcome the effects of some really negative humans that were there before you came along. Show patience to the Pit Bull that is more aloof than you would like; the dog may have developed that aloofness as a defense mechanism against aspects in its former life.
- **Trust.** While it may seem obvious that the bonding process would involve trust, remember that adult Pit Bulls may have never learned that they can trust a human, or they may have learned that trust is transitory, that sometimes they could trust and sometimes they couldn't. Be the human that your adult Pit Bull can *always* trust.

111

■ **Reward.** A good way to build a bond with a neglected or abused Pit Bull is to positively reinforce, not just their accomplishing something in house-training or basic training; reinforce when the Pit Bull clearly shows that it is beginning to bond with you. That might be when it doesn't flinch when you walk up or if you are standing somewhere and the dog comes up to you.

It is most gratifying that many adult Pit Bulls become thoroughly bonded with their new homes and their new humans. Your adult Pit Bull may not be mentally aware of its chance at a good new life, at least not mentally aware the way a human being would be, but many dog lovers bear witness that a rescued dog seems to know that it has been just that—*rescued*. Many Pit Bulls being rehomed out of very dire circumstances seem to be the canine equivalent of overjoyed to be in a safe and loving new environment.

Training the Adult Pit Bull

Many rescued Pit Bulls may have had little or no positive training. Adult Pit Bulls need to have the same basic lessons that a Pit Bull puppy should have. Following the training approach for Pit Bull puppies (pages 73 to 90) you can, with maybe a little more time and a lot more patience, achieve some surprising results. Adult Pit Bulls, like puppy Pit Bulls, want to please an owner with whom they have thoroughly bonded. The key thing a human must do, for either an adult or a puppy,

is to find a way to let the animal know what it is you want. Usually a Pit Bull that understands what is required will eventually be able to do it.

Some differences between puppies and adults may exist when the adult Pit Bull has previously belonged to someone who tried to do some training and failed. You can well imagine if the rescued dog was physically punished when it didn't sit correctly that training the dog to *sit* might dredge up bad memories for the dog. As with socialization, keep a diary or journal every time you observe some reluctance or some hesitation that seems based on previous experience. Paying attention to special needs that your Pit Bull may demonstrate will help you make your training fit the dog, instead of the dog having to fit the training.

Treats as a Reward Revisited

Another difference may appear in the reward given for successfully obeying. While I don't personally train puppies with food treats, preferring to use praise, tasty treats may be a great idea when working with an adult Pit Bull. Since most Pit Bulls that become adoptable have probably not been given much training and perhaps not even adequate care, reasonable use—still don't overdo it—of treats might speed up the training process. Always use a lot of praise with the treats when you reward a dog. Strangely, the praise in a rehomed dog may be the element most lacking in its former existence.

Professional Help

Some breed advocates believe that owning an adult Pit Bull may be preferable to owning a Pit Bull puppy, if you have never owned a dog before, I would concur with this view, if, and only if, you get professional help, preferably professional help that is experienced with one or more of the Pit Bull breeds.

As with Pit Bull puppies, obedience classes, professional trainers, and Pit Bull rescue groups can provide assistance with special concerns. You should always be in the process of building a brain trust of people you know and can depend upon for sound advice about your Pit Bull. The rescue group or animal shelter from which you adopted your Pit Bull can be of great help.

Offering treats is one way to reinforce obedient behavior in your Pit Bull.

Training a Special Needs Pit Bull

1. All the training in the world will not replace a good collar and leash on a Pit Bull when that collar and leash is in the owner's firm grip. Pit Bulls should never be allowed to run free.
2. Don't expect, as many people do, that you can turn your Pit Bull over to a trainer and come back later for the fully trained dog. Training a dog isn't like dropping a suit off at the dry cleaners and picking it up on the way home. The trainer may be able to get your Pit Bull to do marvelous things, but your Pit Bull doesn't live with your trainer. The dog lives with you! When training fails it is generally not the dog's or professional trainer's fault.
3. Training is never finished. Dogs need to have everyday positive reinforcement and practice in their basic commands.
4. Training needs to be a priority in your household. Each person needs to know what the dog has been taught, how it was taught, and how not to undo what it was taught.

11

Possible Paths for Your Pit Bull

Canine Good Citizen Certificate

What a neat idea, to take the world's most berated and smeared dog and get a legitimate certificate attesting to the dog's positive characteristics. Becoming a Canine Good Citizen is a laudable goal for every dog and a great chance at some vindication for the Pit Bull.

Just What Is a Canine Good Citizen?

Just as the name implies, this is a dog that is well mannered and obedient, and that acts with a strong sense of good behavior. The Canine Good Citizen can be walked by his or her owner without attempting to drag the human down the street. The Canine Good Citizen doesn't bristle and growl at the presence of another dog walking down the same street.

At home the Canine Good Citizen doesn't rush to the front door every time there is a knock or the doorbell rings. The postal worker doesn't live in dread of delivering mail to the house where a Canine Good Citizen lives. In the home,

the Canine Good Citizen behaves and doesn't go into paroxysms of exuberance when visitors come to call. Neither does this paragon of canine virtue jump all over guests. The Canine Good Citizen is a dog of decorum and discipline. Can a Pit Bull aspire to such lofty heights of canine perfection? Certainly, and many have.

Author's note: The CGC is a minimum set of good manners that any dog should have. Unfortunately they don't always translate to good home behavior.

The Canine Good Citizen Certificate is not just a piece of paper you can get like a doctorate from a diploma mill. Perfecting the skills necessary to achieve the Certificate will require some real attention to training detail. Canine Good Citizen training should never take the place of good regular training, but it certainly can pave the way for other kinds of training: obedience trials, agility, flyball, and Animal Assisted Therapy (AAT).

This program began in the late 1980s with acceptance by the American Kennel Club. It has become extremely popular and marks a very positive return to the idea that dogs aren't just for appearances. The CGC has allowed dogs of all kinds of backgrounds to show just how well behaved they can be.

There are many alternatives open to the well-trained Pit Bull and the well-schooled owner. Just one of these is involvement in conformation dog shows.

How the CGC Works

The CGC is not a competition, but a way to get noteworthy attention for a well-behaved dog. Dogs are evaluated on ten different exercises, all of which have very practical applications. This is not a "who gets the most points" kind of testing; the Pit Bull either passes or fails. These are the CGC exercises:

CGC Exercise 1: Accepting a Friendly Stranger

Since control is such a pivotal part of Pit Bull ownership, this exercise is a great check for how you've done in the control area. This exercise demonstrates how well your Pit Bull responds when a nonthreatening and friendly person, such as the CGC evaluator, walks up to you on the "street." The evaluator stops, talks with you, and shakes hands with you and ignores the Pit Bull. Your dog, to pass this exercise must not display any aggressiveness such as growling or barking when the evaluator strolls up in a friendly way.

This exercise can be part of a puppy's regular learning. Get several friends you don't often see—people the Pit Bull does not know—to play the friendly stranger routine over a period of several weeks. Keep your Pit Bull under control and reinforce positive behavior with rewards. The

dog can learn this and it has legitimate everyday value to you and your Pit Bull.

CGC Exercise 2: Sitting Politely for Petting

This exercise is simple; it demonstrates that your Pit Bull is a well-mannered dog. With your dog in the *sit* position on either side of you, the evaluator will approach and pet the dog on head and body. The evaluator will then walk completely around you and your Pit Bull. To pass this test, your dog cannot show aggressiveness or shyness. This exercise can be taught early and is nothing that you should not expect out of your Pit Bull.

CGC Exercise 3: Appearance and Grooming

This time the evaluator will walk up to you and your Pit Bull to see if the dog is healthy, clean, and well groomed. The evaluator will lightly comb or brush your dog, look into its ears, and pick up each foot for inspection. Your Pit Bull can be in a *sit* position or be standing next to you. (You can verbally talk with the dog to reassure him during this part of the CGC.) This is again an exercise best taught early, using strangers to the dog to go through the routine of the exercise.

CGC Exercise 4: Out for a Walk (Walking on a Loose Leash)

Again, this exercise demonstrates the control you have over your Pit Bull. This is not like the formal *heel* position and the Pit Bull can be on either side of you, but you must have him under leash control. You will be given directions by the evaluator to turn left, turn right, reverse your steps, and stop. Again, you are encouraged to reassure your Pit Bull during this

> **Pit Bits:** *Temperament Testing and Canine Good Citizen Testing are worthy goals for all Pit Bull owners. Ironically, even with all the bad press about these dogs, Pit Bulls often do very well in both of these endeavors.*

walk/exercise. This is another fairly simple lesson that can be taught to a youngster.

CGC Exercise 5: Walking Through a Crowd

Your Pit Bull should have learned this lesson fairly early in life. This exercise is simply walking your Pit Bull alongside three people, some of whom are accompanied by their dogs. Your Pit Bull can show natural interest in the other people and the other dogs, but not shy or aggressive behavior.

CGC Exercise 6: Sit and Down on Command/Staying in Place

Another control exercise that requires you to do several things: (a) Give the *sit* command, (2) Followed by the *down* command. The next part comes while your Pit Bull is on a 20-foot (6.1-m) leash that you hold on to. This part tests just how much control you have over your Pit Bull as you walk away. It tests your dog's ability to obey the *stay* command as you walk to the end of the long leash.

CGC Exercise 7: Coming When Called

This exercise of the CGC test shows your Pit Bull's degree of obedience to you when you give the *come* command.

(1) You give the *stay* command and walk 10 feet (3 m) away. (2) You then turn to face your Pit Bull and give the *come* command. You may clap your hands or use "come-to-me" gestures, (3) The evaluator may distract your Pit Bull by petting him.

CGC Exercise 8: Reaction to Another Dog

This is a tough one for some Pit Bulls, but they can do it. (1) With your dog on a leash, walk across the room or sidewalk. You meet a stranger with a well-behaved dog on his leash, (2) Stop and talk with the stranger, (3) Then walk on for another 15 feet (4.6 m). This exercise allows your Pit Bull to notice the other dog, but you must remain in control. This entire exercise should be part of your Pit Bull's regular repertoire that it learned very early.

CGC Exercise 9: Reacting to Distractions

This CGC exercise tests your Pit Bull's confidence. The evaluator may choose from several distractions, such as slamming doors or suddenly opening doors, both of which are done for the sound distraction. A book may be dropped from a height of several feet or so, flat onto the floor behind your Pit Bull. The evaluator might tip over a chair within 8 feet (3 m) of your dog. You and your Pit Bull may be asked to walk past some loud people that are slapping each other on the shoulders or backs.

Another part of this distraction exercise tests your Pit Bull's reaction to visual distraction. A bike rider or a shopping cart pusher will come between 6 feet (2 m) for the bicyclist and 10 feet (3 m) for the rattling shopping cart. A distraction might be a jogger passing in front of you and your Pit Bull. It might also be a person with a walker, crutches, or a wheelchair walking in front of you. All of these variations on the kind of people your Pit Bull might encounter should have been built into your socialization of your dog.

CGC Exercise 10: Supervised Separation

This part of the GCG test demonstrates how well your Pit Bull can be left alone for a period of three minutes without becoming excessively agitated or panicking. Your Pit Bull will be on a 6-foot (1.8-m) leash. You will hand this leash to the evaluator and leave your dog's field of vision for three minutes. A passing grade for this is given when your Pit Bull neither chews or tugs on the leash, barks, whines, or paces.

All of these exercises should be part of what your Pit Bull has learned. It must be admitted that starting puppies off early in a regimen that includes all of these exercises will probably be easier than teaching these characteristics of a Canine Good Citizen to a rescued adult Pit Bull. That certainly does not mean that it is impossible or even unlikely for your rescued dog to achieve the CGC certificate. It does mean that you had better be really on your dog trainer toes with an adult over a puppy.

Your Pit Bull should be taught how to walk on a loose leash when she is a puppy.

Obedience Trials

Not every dog that is obedience trained is a candidate for obedience trials. Most dogs, even most Pit Bulls—unless they have aggression problems—can complete the Novice portion. These trials and matches are both challenging and enjoyable for many Pit Bulls and their owners. Both the AKC and the UKC have their own, very similar versions of obedience trials and the degrees that can be conferred on a dog of the Pit Bull breeds. There are different echelons or levels of obedience trials, but, in the highest levels,

they generally include jumping, retrieving, scent work, and off-leash work.

AKC Obedience Titles

You and your dog have a real chance to learn how to work together if you pursue an obedience title or degree. AKC Obedience Trials are often held in conjunction with AKC dog shows. You and your dog can work up the obedience trial ladder by competing in the different classes. (The word "class" here describes the level of the competition and not an actual training class.)

1. **Novice A and Novice B Classes.** For dogs six months and older that have NOT won a Companion Dog (CD) title.
    Novice exercises are: *heel* on leash and figure eight; *stand* for examination, *heel* free (off leash), *recall*, long *sit*, and long *down*.
2. **Companion Dog (CD) Title.** Awarded to a dog that has received qualifying scores licenses (or Member) obedience trials, under three different judges, if there were at least six dogs competing in each of the three obedience trials.
3. **Open A Class.** For dogs that have won a CD, but have not yet progressed to the Companion Dog Excellent (CDX). The dog's owner or a member of the family must handle the dog, not a professional handler.
4. **Open B Class.** For dogs that have earned a CD title or a CDX title or a Utility Dog (UD) title. The owner or anyone else can handle in this class.
    Open Class exercises are: *heel* free and figure eight; *drop* on *recall*;

retrieve on flat; *retrieve* over high jump; *retrieve* over broad jump; long *sit*; and long *down*.

5. **AKC The Companion Dog Excellent (CDX) Degree.** May be awarded by the AKC to a dog that has received qualifying scores at three obedience trials under three different judges.

6. **AKC Utility A Class.** This class is for dogs that have earned their CDX, but not the Utility Dog (UD) title. The dog's owner or a member of the family must handle the dog.

7. **AKC Utility B Class.** For dogs that have won either the CDX or UD title. Anyone can handle the dog in this class.

    Utility exercises are: a signal exercise scent discrimination, article 1; scent discrimination, article 2; directed *retrieve*; moving *stand* and examination; and directed jumping.

8. **AKC Utility Dog (UD) Title.** This is awarded to the dog that has received qualifying scores in three different trials under three different judges.

    Utility dogs may earn points toward the Obedience Trial Championship or OTCh.

9. **AKC Utility Dog Excellent (UDX) Title.** Awarded to dogs that have earned qualifying scores at ten separate AKC obedience events! These scores must be in Open B and Utility B classes and some other specific criteria for awarding the UDX.

It is easy to see that your dog and you have some real work ahead of you if obedience trials are what you choose to pursue. It is important to remember that every

college football player does not become an All-American selection. Likewise, not every well-trained American Staffordshire Terrier, Bull Terrier, or Staffordshire Bull Terrier has the capacity to go all the way to UDX or OTCh. That does not mean that you and your pet are of lesser value. It has been my experience that many people in obedience trials have made a conscious decision that the trials and all the training that leads up to entering these trials are going to be a significant part of their, and their dog's, lifestyle. That lifestyle is admirable, but it is not for every dog or for every dog owner.

The best way to deal with all the obedience trial information and requirements is to deal with obedience in the same way that the man who decided to eat an elephant dealt with this large undertaking—one bite at a time. The AKC obedience events are designed—as are the United Kennel Club and the Canadian Kennel Clubs similar programs—to be in a logical progression. If your dog does well on the lower rungs of the obedience trial ladder, then move up to the next level, until you and your dog have gone as far as it seems practical to go. For this book, I call this reaching of a good place to stop, *"The Pitter Principle."*

The best way to approach training for obedience trials is to contact the American Kennel Club for Amstaff, Staffybulls, and Bull Terriers for specific information about what is required and where trials in your area may be scheduled. Again, if you have faithfully trained your pet, the first steps on the obedience ladder are not that big a stretch from the training you have already done.

UKC Obedience Titles

Much like the AKC (but they would hate to admit it), the United Kennel Club has a strong slate of obedience titles that are open to American Pit Bull Terriers and the other Pit Bull breeds. These titles must be earned successively, and no obedience titles from the AKC or any other organizations may be substituted for UKC titles.

- **UKC United Companion Dog (UCD) Title.** This title must be won from the A or B divisions of the Novice Class. There can be any combination of A or B qualifying scores. To earn the UCD, the Pit Bull must earn three qualifying scores at three different UKC-licensed obedience trials under at least *two* different UKC-licensed obedience judges.
- **UKC United Companion Dog Excellent (UCDX) Title.** A Pit Bull must already have earned the UCD title *before* it is eligible to earn legs toward the UCDX. The UCDX must be earned from any combination of qualifying scores from the A or B divisions of the Open Class. To earn the UCDX, a Pit Bull must earn three qualifying scores at three different UKC-licensed obedience trials under at least two different UKC-licensed obedience trial judges.
- **UKC United Utility Dog (UUD) Title.** A Pit Bull must already have earned the UCDX title *before* it is eligible to earn legs toward the UUD. The UUD title must be earned in any combination of qualifying score from the A or B Utility Class. As with the other UKC obedience titles, the UUD is earned by three qualifying scores at three different UKC-licensed obedience trails under at least

two different UKC-licensed obedience trial judges.

- **UKC United Obedience Champion Dog (UOCH) Title.** A Pit Bull must earn the UUD before it is eligible to earn points/legs toward the UOCH. To earn the UOCH, a Pit Bull must meet all the following requirements:
  1. combined wins, at five different UKC-licensed trials, and
  2. a qualifying score in each of the Open B and Utility B classes in the same trial, with a combined score of 370 or above.

The UKC obedience ladder is somewhat different from the AKC version, but it is obvious that neither of these organizations have designed their obedience title quest to be a cakewalk. (I have included the UKC at length because of the AKC's different breed recognition elements.) The UKC obedience titles are not always listed in relation to the dog's name in the same way as the AKC obedience titles; UKC titles come at the beginning of the dog's name!

The United Kennel Club allows members of AMBOR (the American Mixed Breed Obedience Registry) to participate in some UKC activities. For the Pit Bulls from mixed or crossed heritage, the UKC has some options.

Other Kennel Clubs and Obedience

The Canadian Kennel Club (CKC). The CKC is a strong and active North American registry. The CKC has a thriving obedience program that is somewhat similar to that of the American Kennel Club. It is interesting that the Canadian equivalent of the Canine Good Citizen program is called the Canine Good Neighbour program.

Animal-Assisted Therapy (AAT)

There is probably no more rewarding experience than when our pets bring pleasure and comfort to others. While there are several animal therapy organizations, the Delta Society is one of the oldest and largest animal therapy organizations. Animal-Assisted Therapy (AAT) is more than putting your Pit Bull in the family sedan and driving over to a nursing home or hospital. AAT is provided under the auspices of a health/human service professional with a specific clinical goal for a specific individual.

Author's note: There is a great degree of difference between dogs used for therapeutic visits to nursing homes and the like and specially trained dogs that are service animals that assist persons with certain disabilities.

The Delta Society defines AAT as "…a goal-oriented intervention in which an animal is an integral part of the treatment process." Other Delta Society material gives the following definition of service animals: Service animals, as defined by the Americans with Disabilities Act (Federal Code of Regulations, 1990), are individually trained to do work or perform tasks for the benefit of a person with a disability, a physical or mental impairment that substantially limits one

> **Pit Bits:** Many Pit Bulls excel as AAT (Animal-Assisted Therapy) animals. Seeing one's Pit Bull bring joy to an autistic child or to a nursing home resident is a great experience.

or more of the major life activities of the individual. Federal law permits qualified people, who have disabilities, to be accompanied by their service animals in all places of public accommodation, including places with posted "No pets" policies. Service animals are not considered "pets."

Many Pit Bulls are ideal for this sort of help for humans. To be an actual visiting dog your Pit Bull must earn a therapy certificate from a national organization with that responsibility. Your pet must pass a test not entirely unlike the Canine Good Citizen Certificate training to specifically assess your dog's ability to relate to and interact with disabled or injured people.

It is mandated that you and your pet be thoroughly reviewed and screened before any sort of visiting involvement is considered. Obedience clubs, the AKC, the UKC, and other organizations are providing screening and training to dogs that meet the temperament and behavioral qualifications for an AAT dog. If your Pit Bull has the stability and personality for therapy work or to become a service animal, sincerely consider the contribution that your dog could make to humans in need.

There are a number of service and therapy dog organizations. One of these is TDI—Therapy Dogs International.

121

12 Pleasurable Activities with Your Pit Bull

Understanding Kennel Clubs and the Pit Bull Breeds

There are many fun and challenging activities for you and your Pit Bull. Many of these, like conformation dog shows, are held under the auspices of some national kennel club or similar organization. Not all of the Pit Bull breeds and kindred dogs are welcomed by all the kennel clubs. It is therefore important to look at who admits whom in the dog world.

1. **The American Kennel Club (AKC).** American Staffordshire Terriers, Staffordshire Bull Terriers, Bull Terriers (White, Colored, and Miniature);
2. **The United Kennel Club (UKC).** American Pit Bull Terriers, American Bulldogs, Bull Terriers (White, Colored, and Miniature) Staffordshire Bull Terriers.
3. **The American Dog Breeders Show, Inc. (ADBSI).** The ADBSI is an exclusively American Pit Bull Terrier registry with the credo "To insure the continued existence of the APBT breed today and for generations to come." The

ADBSI also wants to educate the general public about the American Pit Bull Terrier and its owners. Responsible dog ownership is also a key goal for this organization.

Like the AKC and the UKC, the American Dog Breeders Show, Inc. conducts conformation dog shows. Like the UKC, the ADBSI sponsors weight pulls but only for American Pit Bull Terriers.

Conformation Dog Shows

Dog shows have long been the hallmark of dog registries and breed clubs. These shows are more than exhibitions of beautiful specimens of particular breeds of dogs. Dog shows allow dog-by-dog evaluation not necessarily against the other dogs of the same breed, but against the written "standard" for each breed.

Dog show judges, operating under licensure or certification of the large kennel club organizations, such as the AKC and the UKC, must carefully study the standards of the breeds that they are approved to judge. Becoming a judge is a fairly long and involved process that tests a judging candidate's knowledge of the written standard and the ability to visualize the meaning of the written words in the living dogs of that breed. Judges have to serve a type of apprenticeship before they are approved and licensed.

In a conformation dog show the judges carefully go over each entrant to see to how close each is to exemplifying the written and approved breed Standard. It is, in the opinion of the judge, the dog that comes closest to the description in the standard that wins. Dogs within a breed are judged in several categories or classes, including by age and by gender. All the class winners are then judged to determine the best of breed.

Once a dog has won best of its breed, it competes against the other best of breeds in the other breeds within its Group. An American Staffordshire Terrier, (let's call him Bullster of Bull Run) that won best of breed (best Amstaff), for example, would then compete with all the terriers that were best in their breeds. If Bullster of Bull Run is best terrier, or best of Group, as it is called, he would then compete with all the other winners of all the other groups—Herding, Sporting, Hounds, etc. If Bullster is judged to be the closest to being the ideal of the American Staffordshire Terrier standard than any of the other dogs of the other groups are to their standards, Bullster wins and is declared Best in Show (BiS).

Points

When a dog wins at the breed level that dog is given a certain number of points.

> **Pit Bits:** *Some American Pit Bull Terriers have been double-registered as American Staffordshire Terriers. One such great conformation show dog was the top American Kennel Club's Amstaff the same year that he won as the top United Kennel Club's APBT.*

These points are based on the number of dogs that this winner has had to defeat. The Winners Dog and the Winners Bitch (the best nonchampion male and female) can also receive points. There are three kinds of shows, using the AKC as an example, where this winning Amstaff can gain points: all-breed shows, specialty shows (for Amstaffs only), group shows, in this case for all the terrier breeds. When this American Staffordshire Terrier, Bullster (or an American Pit Bull Terrier in the UKC) accumulates enough points the dog is awarded the title of Champion and Bullster of Bull Run is now CH. Bullster of Bull Run.

Championships are serious business in the dog-breeding world. Bullster can, as a champion, expect to be in some demand as a stud dog. If Bullster had been a female, champion stud dogs would be more likely to want to breed to a champion female. Breeders believe that it is much easier to have top-quality puppies produced when both the sire and the dam are proven winners. The more top-quality offspring a stud dog sires, the more he will be in demand as a stud dog and consequently, the higher his stud fee will be.

How to Learn About Dog Shows and Showing Your Dog

■ **Visit a lot of dog shows.** The best way to understand how dog shows work is to attend as many as possible. One hint on visiting dog shows: Go early; many shows are over in the early afternoon, especially on Sundays, the last day of many shows. If you want to see a particular breed, go early.

■ **Ask questions.** While dog shows are busy events, there is always an opportunity to chat with people while they are grooming their dogs or have finished for the day.

■ **Leave your dog at home.** A dog show is not the place to socialize a shaky Pit Bull. This is especially true for young puppies, which are usually not allowed at dog shows.

■ **Read the standard.** Read the standard of the Pit Bull breed that interests you. Read it carefully and try to visualize the dog described. You can get a copy of the standard from many breed books or from the breed club or from the kennel club.

■ **Observe the judges.** See how each judge approaches the task of deciding which entrant is closest to its standard. Hopefully you have read the standard by this point, and you might agree with the judge and you might not; however, don't try to talk to the judge about your opinions!

■ **Observe the exhibitors.** See how they "stack"—get their dogs to stand in a way that best shows their conformation—

their dogs and watch how they run and walk their dogs so that the dogs always look their best for the judge. Notice how the exhibitors or their handlers are dressed, even down to the color outfits they have on that will complement their dogs' appearance.

■ **Observe the dogs.** See how well trained they are and how many dogs seem to have a little more zip or charisma when they are being judged. By looking at dogs, especially the winners, you can begin to have an idea about how your Pit Bull should look if he is to become a show dog.

■ **Experience the drama of the show ring.** You can do this even if breeds that don't interest you are being judged. Learn from all sources. You may see something in the judging of another breed that may help you.

■ **Watch the sportsmanship.** See how the other dogs' owners and handlers congratulate the winner. Even if they don't always mean it, it looks good.

■ **Watch how the winner acts.** It seems as if many show dogs understand exactly what has just happened and that they won!

■ **Remember that all the dogs and all the owners have won.** Think of the thousands upon thousand of dogs that never had an opportunity to be entered in a dog show. Imagine how good it looks for the Pit Bull breeds to have dogs in full view of the public with no fighting or attacking of other dogs.

■ **Have a good time.** Dog shows can be a lot of fun. You'll see people that like the same kinds of dogs that you do. You can buy needed items at the ven-

Showing the immense drive and power of the Pit Bull, this contestant in a weight-pull competition pulls because he wants to, not because he is forced to do so.

dor booths. You may find someone that you can correspond with or converse with about issues confronting you and your Pit Bull.

Weight-Pulling Contests

Both American Dog Breeders and Show, Inc. and the United Kennel Club have weight-pull events. The ADBSI confines its weight pulls to American Pit Bull Terriers. Interestingly, in the UKC, any breed of dog from the tiniest to the largest can compete.

Pit Bits: *Weight pulling is an excellent competition event for Pit Bulls. Not only do they have an opportunity to show off their incredible strength, but training and competing help to burn off a lot of excess energy.*

Weight pulls are good contests for the Pit Bull breeds. In these contests, dogs have a chance to do something they obviously enjoy. Placed in a harness attached to a weighted vehicle that is either on wheels, on rails, or on snow,

Pit Bulls excel at weight-pull contests.

dogs seem to get a big charge out of the entire atmosphere. Contestants are judged on how much weight they can pull and by the proportion of their body weight to the amount of weight they can pull.

Some uninitiated persons might think that weight pulls are, in some way, cruel to the dogs involved. Nothing is further from the truth! The owner cannot touch the dog in any way, but can shout encouragement from the finish line. If the weight pulling was cruel, all the dog has to do is to stop pulling. I once saw a medium-sized Pit Bull pull a Nissan pickup truck loaded to the top of the truck bed with dog food. The load had to be over 1,000 pounds (680 kg) and the dog was very enthusiastic about pulling it. She pulled it about 20 feet (6.1 m) on a concrete floor—the dog was on a traction-providing carpet—and seemed to enjoy the cheers of the crowd.

IWPA

A nonprofit organization that promotes the sport of weight pulls by dogs is the International Weight Pull Association

(IWPA) which holds sanctioned events throughout locations in North America. This organization touts not only the fun of the weight pulls themselves, but also the fact that such events are supportive of the working heritage of many kinds of dogs. Like the UKC, the IWPA is open to all dogs.

IWPA weight pulls are only with wheeled carts on earthen surfaces or sleds on snow. Dogs compete within their own weight class, of which there are eight: 0–20#, 21–40#, 41–60#, 61–80#, 81–100#, 101–125#, 126–150#, 151#, and over. Again, the owner or handler has no physical contact with the dog during the actual pull. The weight must be pulled 16 feet (4.8 m) within one minute. Ties are broken by the dog with the quickest time to 16 feet being the winner. The IWPA also stresses that this event encourages good canine physical condition. The IWPA is justifiably proud of the fact that no dog has been injured in one of their events since the organization was founded in 1984.

Agility Competitions

Agility events are a combination of good training, owner-dog verbal interaction, and flat-out speed. The canine entrant is directed by voice commands from its owner through an ever-changeable course. The course consists of obstacles, jumps, tunnels, swaying bridges (UKC only), and platforms (AKC only), where the dog is required to wait until given the command to proceed. All of this excitement-packed activity is timed against an official clock.

Many people are surprised by the fact that Pit Bulls can be trained to be effective tracking dogs.

Agility scoring is done by judges who make sure the dog does each obstacle as the rules specify. As in weight pulls, the dog's owner cannot touch nor have any other physical contact. Agility is fast-paced, but even more importantly, it is a real test of the training and the relationship between the dog and the human.

Schutzhund (VPG)

Many dog owners, if they even know the word "*Schutzhund,*" picture only a German Shepherd Dog biting the arm of a well-padded person that somewhat resembles the Michelin Tire Man. Schutzhund or as it is now called, VPG *Vielseitigkeitspruefung fur Gebrauchshunde*, or roughly translated to mean "*versatility test for working dogs*" began in Germany in 1903 as a way to test the working skills of dogs. In Germany, dogs that are to be used for breeding in certain breeds cannot get by on good looks alone. They must have the necessary behavior and abilities to be guard, police, or protection animals *before* they are allowed to be bred. Beginning with German Shepherd Dogs, VPG now has many breeds in many countries involved. Some of the Pit Bull breeds have excelled at this oft-misunderstood sport.

Many Pit Bulls have done very well in the world of Schutzhund (or VPG) training, an area of endeavor long the domain of the German breeds.

Protection

The third part of Schutzhund or VPG is protection. It is this component that is most misunderstood. The important aspect of this phase is understanding the relationship between the dog and its handler. Biting the guy in the padded suit—called a trial helper—must never happen, unless the dog or the handler is attacked, then the VPG dog must attack immediately and without hesitation. The more important part of this response is that the dog must also *stop* attacking immediately, on command. The dog then guards the attacker in the padded suit without showing any further aggression.

The Pit Bull breeds can be trained to be quite proficient at VPG events. There are three levels that a dog can attain in Schutzhund; SCH I, SCH II, and SCH III. Some Pit Bulls have reached the highest level. If you are interested in this and several other similar training sports, you should contact the DVG America Group nearest your home.

Tracking

Many people think that VPG is about training attack dogs. That is not the entire truth. There are three specific areas that are tested in VPG work. The first of these is tracking. The dog must be able to track footsteps over difficult ground, change direction without getting off the track in the least, and spot dropped items and alert the handler to the presence of these items.

Obedience

The second element of VPG is obedience. In a way very similar to AKC and UKC obedience trials, VPG dogs must do many exercises both on and off the leash. Interesting, the *sit*, the *down*, and the *stand* are done in VPG, but they are done while the dog is moving!

Other Fun Activities for You and Your Pit Bull

Anyone who has ever taken the time, or has had the opportunity, to get to know a Pit Bull knows full well that many of these dogs are clowns. Because of this type of personality, you can find many fun things for your Pit Bull and you to do. Some of these you and the dog can make up as you go along, but there are some other activities that you can check out to see if they might be right for you and your dog:

- **FlyBall.** This sport is a team relay sport in which dogs compete, as quickly as possible against another team of dogs. (Dogs involved in FlyBall must ignore the opposing team.) FlyBall is one of the most exciting of all the things that dogs can be taught to do. Dogs speed down a lane, clearing hurdles as they go. At the end of the lane they pounce on a box that fires out a ball that the dog has to catch in its mouth. When they have the ball they reverse engines and run back up the lane to give the ball to their waiting owner. The object is for a team of dogs to get as many balls as possible in the least amount of time. (Check out *flyball.org*.)
- **DockDog.** This activity's name probably explains most of what the activity is about. Spawned by retriever owners, DockDog competitions are attracting a surprising number of Pit Bull people. This is a great sport for the Pit Bull that likes jumping into water—judging is done of the greatest distance of the jumps—and also likes retrieving things back to the owner and doing it all over again.

Pit Bull Activities to Avoid

In the United States, a group of "sportsmen" have found an uplifting new pastime: they match dogs with hogs. This is not Porky versus Pluto; these purveyors of combativeness usually use American Bulldogs, though some larger Pit Bulls are often used. Most of the hogs are not the famed Russian boars that might stand a better chance; these hogs are often regular barnyard pigs that get chewed up by their canine opponents.

There are also some Pit Bulls, Pit Bull mixes, Plott Hound/Pit Bull crosses that are used in feral hog hunting in several states. It is even possible, if you have enough money and not much humanity, to be taken along on one of these hunts. Some lucky hunters even get to shoot the hog that has been cornered by a pack of dogs.

The Pit Bull breeds may do well in battling other creatures. Pit Bulls and Airedales were often included in bear hound packs and mountain lion packs. The hounds find the bears or lions and the terriers keep the prey occupied until the hunter arrives to do the shooting. Ask yourself if these are the kinds of activities that you want to choose for your Pit Bull. Dogs that engage in such activities are more like the pit dogs that are so aggressive around other animals that they are often put to sleep because they do not usually make the best choices for family pets.

13 Polishing Your Pit Bull: Beyond the Basics

Many Pit Bulls are among the greatest clowns and comedians in dogdom. There are several basic tricks that can be fun to teach a Pit Bull and can have the added value of disarming people that see these dogs only in the severest of lights.

Speak/Quiet

Some dog owners are reluctant to try this command because they are afraid that it gives a Pit Bull *carte blanche* to bark too much. These fears are unjustified, for teaching a dog to bark on command has with it a cut-off valve that lets the dog know when to shut up.

There are all kinds of lead-ins that you can use to make this trick funny and fun. You can simply use the command *speak* to get a bark. You can ask questions that have "yes" and "no" answers and get one bark for "yes" and two for "no." With a little imagination, teaching your Pit Bull to speak can become a very entertaining way of sharing your dog's good qualities with friends, neighbors, and others.

Speak also has some useful aspects. Knowing where your pet is in the dark is as simple as a verbal command. In the case of an emergency you can use this command to signal to others where you and your pet are. Again, the ability to teach your Pit Bull to vocalize may come in handy for many reasons.

Depending on your training style, you can give a simple verbal command, or, if you developed hand signals, similar to those used with deaf Pit Bulls, you can secretly (to all but you and the Pit Bull) get your pet to vocalize. Here's how to teach *speak;* you can add your variations on this theme as you wish:

1. Begin with a nonbarking dog; you want to teach Bullster to bark when you want him to bark, not for any other reason.
2. Discover something that makes Bullster bark for a happy reason. Perhaps you withhold a treat or a toy and tease the dog as in the beginning of playtime. Keep the moment fun and not in the traditional "training is all business" mode.

Contrary to what many people think, teaching your dog to "speak" on command is not a bad idea.

3. When you have discovered something that makes Bullster want to bark, watch him and anticipate when a bark is coming. Just as he is about to bark, give your verbal command: "*Speak*" or "*Talk*" or whatever word you want to be the cue for this command.

4. Praise and reward, with a food treat, Bullster for the bark, even if it is a little half-bark. This step can be repeated until Bullster clearly understands that he earns a treat reward and praise only for the barks that are responses to your verbal command.

5. After you have the verbal command working, teach Bullster a hand signal, which can be as subtle as touching your left ear or as flamboyant as making the tapping yourself on the side of the head in the "think" gesture. It is important after you have chosen the signal that you gradually wean Bullster away from the verbal command until the hand signal, clicker noise, or whatever cue you use is the only cue Bullster gets that will get him a treat reward and praise for barking.

6. The *stop* or *release* cue is "*Quiet,*" "*Hush,*" or whatever word you choose. This command is taught just like the *speak*. You have to make sure Bullster knows that "*Quiet*" is the cue for not

barking and that by not barking he gets a reward.

7. You again start when Bullster is quiet. You signal for a speak and reward the barking.

8. Just as you did with *speak*, you can now add a hand signal cue for *"Quiet."* If your hand signal is a traditional *"Shhh"* index finger across your lips or the knifelike move of your finger across your throat, or some other gesture, make sure that Bullster sees it and comes to understand it means a *no bark* and a reward. Don't reward any bark that comes after the *quiet* signal has been given.

To make *speak* and *quiet* work don't reward any barking that you have not commanded or signaled. Don't let that sneaky Bullster try to trick you into rewarding him for a bark when he wants a treat. Make sure the other members of your home don't fall for Bullster's trick either.

Delayed Gratification

This is an excellent command to teach Bullster. It does double duty as an entertaining trick that wins friends and admirers for the well-trained dog. It also highlights that a Pit Bull such as Bullster is under control and is a very disciplined pet. There are several ways to teach *delayed gratification*, which is my name for this trick and which seems a little classier than the "Dog Biscuit on the Nose" trick. For Bullster, and for novice dog trainers and Pit Bull owners, the commands will be ver-

bal and simple. You can add hand signals or clicker techniques after Bullster knows the basic command. Start this command in the sit position.

1. Teach Bullster to remain still and to become comfortable with you gently holding onto his lower jaw. Reward Bullster when he does not move, even if only for a short moment. Do this step repeatedly, over a period of a couple of days or however long it takes, until Bullster feels comfortable and understands that by not moving he will get a treat. In this style of training you will need a command or cue word; *"Hold"* is as good as any.

2. Now that Bullster accepts this remaining still with his lower jaw gently in your grasp, begin to move a dog biscuit in an ever so slow movement toward Bullster's nose. I like dog biscuits for this because they are immediately identifiable to onlookers as to what they are and they are not the training treat I am using to reward in this command. Continue to say, *"Hold"* and reward Bullster if he remains motionless. I do not reward with the same dog biscuit I have been moving toward his noise. That biscuit will be a special treat when Bullster does the entire trick correctly.

3. While Bullster's lower jaw is still in your grasp, slowly move the dog biscuit toward his nose. Saying *"Hold"* as you do, let the dog biscuit come to rest very briefly on Bullster's nose and then take it away and reward with his regular treat.

4. Maintaining the gentle, but firm hold on Bullster's lower jaw, gradually

increase the time that you allow the dog biscuit to remain on his nose. Slowly progress from holding it on Bullster's nose, saying *"Hold"* as you do, until you can begin to let the dog biscuit balance there for ever-increasing increments of time. This step ends when you can leave the biscuit balancing on Bullster's nose for as long as you like. Always reward with the different kind of treat when Bullster remains motionless; always put the dog biscuit away, in a pocket or somewhere.

5. Still saying, *"Hold"* gradually ease away your grip on Bullster's lower jaw. Reward Bullster if he remains motionless while you are not holding his lower jaw. After he remains motionless on this *hold* command, put the dog biscuit back on his nose without letting go of it. Gradually let the dog biscuit come to be solely balanced on Bullster's nose without you holding it there. Reward Bullster for remaining motionless.

6. Bullster now sits motionless on the cue word "hold," balancing the dog biscuit all on his own. Without needlessly prolonging the time of the trick, after balancing the biscuit for 30 seconds or so, build in a release word such as *"OK"* or *"Eat."* Then, and only then, does Bullster get to eat this dog biscuit.

You can build in several variations such as turning your back on Bullster as he is balancing the biscuit. You could even leave the room, but don't leave the poor guy there with the biscuit on his nose for much longer than 30–45 seconds. It is also possible that an athletic Pit Bull can learn to flip the dog biscuit in the air

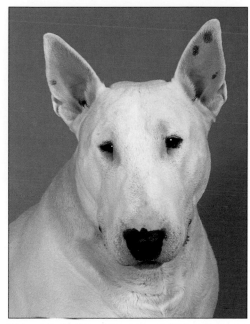

This white Bull Terrier is often mistaken for, or misidentified as, a Pit Bull. With a legacy as more of a show dog than a fighter, the "White Cavalier" has a jaunty, happy terrier personality.

and catch it for a flourish of his own devising.

You can add this wrinkle to the Dog Biscuit on the Nose trick, using the techniques used in clicker training, by waiting until Bullster has caught the dog biscuit before it hits the floor and reinforcing by a click reward when he does catch it.

Find

One clever trick that Bullster can easily learn is a more informal version of some

The miniature Bull Terrier (this is the colored variety) has all the terrier spunk and high energy level. It makes an excellent pet, just as its larger relatives do.

facets of both an obedience trial word and Schutzhund. This trick looks harder than it is and is always entertaining for guests or visitors in your home. This trick also has a useful and perhaps very important aspect naturally built into it. What you want Bullster to do is to, on command, find some other person or member of your family.

This is also a good trick because it can involve all the members of a household. It does take some coordination with other people, some of whom may be children, but that can be handled. *Find* involves teaching Bullster the names of the members of your family; let's start with three children, Catie, Peter, and Julia. Each of

these children understands what we want Bullster to learn and each of them has a dog treat in their pocket.

1. Start this command inside, with all the children standing in line. You want to build Bullster's name into this so that the poor dog doesn't go running off to find someone just because you called their name. The command is always *"Bullster, find _____"* and you put in a name. This first step is simple and may be done over several days. Two of the children know that they are simply to stand still because their name is not going to be in the command. You say Bullster *"Find"* (a brief pause) *"Catie."*

Peter and Julia don't move, but Catie enthusiastically opens her arms and calls Bullster to her and rewards him. Each child gets to be the one to be the object of *find* and each one gets to reward Bullster with a treat. Initially you are staying simply in a room or in the back-yard with the children standing in a line. It is important that the command *"Bull-ster* (which alerts the dog), *find"* (identi-fies what Bullster is to do) name of child, which tells Bullster who he is to find. Each child is to reward the dog in the same way with praise and a treat.

2. The object of the command *find* is behind a tree or some other not really concealed place, but not in the direct line of sight for Bullster. Again, each child gets to be found. They are told not to run from Bullster or make it hard for him to get the reward he has earned.

3. Bullster is told to *find* a child who is actually hiding—not behind closed doors but not in plain sight. Again, each child gets to hide and gets to reward Bullster when he or she is found. Bull-ster is still earning his rewards each time, but the search is getting harder.

4. The searches get gradually harder, until Bullster clearly knows what *"Find"* means and the different names of each of the people in the household. If you have access to a large fenced area or a large building, have the dog find each person.

5. Bullster is now an accomplished *find* dog. You might add the *speak* command, issued by each person and rewarded separately from the *find* reward. Bullster now has a good trick in his repertoire.

Bang! Bang! Play Dead! Is just one of a myriad of tricks a Pit Bull can learn.

He can find each person in the family—or others if you want to add them. Bullster now knows that he can earn rewards for both the *find* and the *speak* to the person found.

Bullster has learned a clever trick and the family has learned, and all of them are part of Bullster's success. Additionally, Bullster's *find* skills can be used not just to show off a trick but to find other persons in the house or yard or in emergencies away from the home.

Bang Play Dead

Bang Play Dead is the classic old trick taught to all kinds of animals. Bullster can learn it without much trouble. *Bang Play*

Pit Bulls have a natural sense of humor and enjoy clownish behavior. There are many tricks that can bring out this fun side in a Pit Bull.

Dead is actually what some trainers call *Roll Over*. It begins in the *down* position from the Five Starter Commands. You teach it like this:

1. Bullster is in a *down*. Using a treat in your right hand, holding the treat under Bullster's nose, you slowly move the treat back toward Bullster's right shoulder toward the middle of his back. Bullster will follow the treat and actually ends up on his back. You could use your other hand to help Bullster complete the rollover.
2. When he is on his back you say *"Bang Play Dead"* and give him the treat. Repeat this step several times until Bullster understands it and knows he has to be on his back to earn the treat.
3. Introduce the hand signal of your finger pointing at Bullster like a gun barrel. Always reward Bullster when he rolls over.
4. Gradually, teach Bullster how to go from a standing position onto his back. Some trainers are able to eliminate the words *"Bang Play Dead"* and just say *"Pow!"* using the hand signal of a gun

and get the same response. Pit Bulls are natural actors and hams and when Bullster really comes to like this command, he'll do it with some style all his own.

Pick a Spot/ Settle In/Crate Up

Pick a spot or *settle in* or *crate up* is another trick that is easy to teach and also very useful in everyday life. Bullster is a great pet, but there are times, even in the life of a great pet, that the dog is in the way or is otherwise bothersome. Not only is this trick amusing for others to see, but it also helps make Bullster a better pet.

Essentially, what you want is for Bullster to find a place and go there and lie down or camp out. You can teach the *pick a spot* or *settle in* like this:

1. Using whichever of these terms you want, take Bullster to the place you want him to be, perhaps his bed or a blanket in a corner or his crate. Once you have Bullster where you want him to be, give him a treat and some toy or chew to occupy him and say, *"Bullster, settle in,"* or *"Bullster, pick a spot."* If you want the Pit Bull to go to his crate, you take him there, leaving the door open, and say *"Crate up"* and reward him and give him something to chew on.
2. **(Alternate)** Perhaps an even easier way to teach Bullster to go to a specific spot is to toss a treat there so that he goes to get it.
3. If Bullster starts to get up from the chosen spot or leave his crate, *"No"* (in your command voice) should suffice

and reward Bullster when he does stay where he should stay. Simply repeat this simple command until Bullster realizes that he earns a treat and toy to chew on if he does what you tell him.

Other Tricks

Your Pit Bull now has amassed a lot of learning. The beautiful thing about dog training is that many basic commands can lead to more elaborate tricks and abilities. The simple training required for the tricks in this chapter were chosen to show how to build on these by finding other entertaining, amusing, and useful things to teach your Pit Bull.

If you can accomplish the Five Starter Commands and the simple tricks in this chapter, you and your Pit Bull can greatly expand your trick inventory. Dogs learn in just the ways that you have seen and read about. Patience, persistence, and timing are the three sedimentary layers on which the careers of Lassie, Rin-tin-tin, Ol' Yeller, and Benji are based.

One thing is common to all these canine stars and many Pit Bulls: The original Lassie (a male named Pal), Ol' Yeller, and Benji were found in animal shelters! All of these stars, like many rescued Pit Bulls, were going nowhere until the right human came along. This book has been about training Pit Bulls, and all the breeds and types that have been branded with that name. There are thousands of dogs of this type needing human beings, human

beings like you to come along and make a difference in their lives. You may never find a Lassie or a Benji, but you could find the best dog that you will ever own and a dog that all the other dogs you have ever known or ever will know will be measured against. You'll never know until you try. Find the right Pit Bull and work hard to be the right owner for that dog!

Breed bans are worthless pieces of legislation that ban a kind of dog without banning a kind of behavior. Ban the deed, not the breed!

Close and consistent human contact makes the Pit Bull a better pet and the human a better pet owner.

Useful Addresses, Web Sites, and Literature

Organizations

The American Kennel Club
260 Madison Avenue
New York, NY 10016
(212) 696-8200
www.akc.org

United Kennel Club
100 E Kilgore Road
Kalamazoo, MI 49002-5584
(269) 343-9020
www.ukcdogs.com

American Dog Breeders Association
(ADBA)
P.O. Box 1771
Salt Lake City, UT 84110
(801) 936-7513

American Mixed Breed Obedience Registry
179 Niblick Road #113
Paso Robles, CA 93446
(805) 226-9275
www.amborusa.org

National American Pit Bull Terrier
Association
210 E. Walnut N.
Baltimore, MD 45872
www.napbt.com

Staffordshire Bull Terrier Club of America
86 Wilson Street
Blauvelt, NY 10913
Staffbullpec@yahoo.com

Staffordshire Terrier Club of America
Lynne Clements, Secretary
P.O. Box 184
Molalla, OR 97038
www.amstaff.org

Bull Terrier Club of America
1122 E. Carol Avenue
Phoenix, AZ 85020-2611
www.btca.com

Miniature Bull Terrier Club of America
251 Stage Road
Nottingham, NH 03290
http://216.157.5.36/mbtca

This handsome blue–brindle American Pit Bull Terrier has the legendary strength of the Pit Bull encased in an outer appearance that makes it a top winner in conformation dog shows.

American College of Veterinary Behaviorists
Department of Small Animal Medicine
Texas A&M University
College Station, TX 77843
www.veterinarybehaviorists.org

American Veterinary Society of Animal Behavior
Avsab@yahoo.com

Animal Behavior Society
Indiana University
2611 East 10th Street
Bloomington, IN 47408
(812) 856-5541
www.animalbehavior.org

Association of Pet Trainers
5096 Sand Road S.E.
Iowa City, IA 52240-8217
(800) PET-DOGS (738-3647)
www.apdt.com

National Association of Dog Obedience Instructors
PMB 369
729 Grapevine Highway
Hurst, TX 76054-2085
www.nadoi.org

Delta Society
875 124th Avenue NE, Suite 101
Bellevue, WA 98005
(425) 226-7357
www.deltasociety.org

AKC Canine Good Citizen Program
Dr. Mary Burch, Director
5580 Centerview Drive
Raleigh, NC 27526
(919) 816-3637
www.akc.org/love/cgc/index.cfm

American Temperament Test Society
P.O. Box 4093
St. Louis, MO 63136
(314) 869-6103
www.atts.org

International Weight Pull Association
1420 N.W. Gilman Boulevard, #2227
Issaquah, WA 98027
www.iwpa.net

North American Dog Agility Council
11550 South Highway 3
Catalda, ID 83810
(208) 682-4309
NADACK9@aol.com

United States Dog Agility Association
P.O. Box 850995
Richardson, TX 75085-0995
(972) 231-9700
www.usdaa.com

Animal Farm Foundation
P.O. Box 624
Bangall, NY 12506
(518) 398-0017
www.animalfarmfoundation.org

Bull Terrier Club of America
Rescue Support Committee
Rescue Hotline: (800) BTBT911
rsc@btca.com

Pit Bull Rescue Central
www.PBRC.net

Spindletop American Pit Bull and
    American Staffordshire Terrier Refuge
PMB 106
10807 Jones Road
Houston, TX 77065
(713) 856-9356
www.spindletoppitbullrefuge.org

Bay Area Doglovers Responsible About
    Pitbulls (BADRAp)
P.O. Box 320776
San Francisco, CA 94132
(510) 414-6471
www.badrap.org

Real Pit Bull
www.realpitbull.com

National American Bulldog Rescue
www.geocities.com/amer.bulldgrescue/

Turtle Moon Rescue, Inc.
P.O. Box 82
Lineville, AL 36266

For Pits Sake
P.O. Box 20790
Castro Valley, CA 94546
(510) 889-PITS (7487)
www.forpitssake.org

With his well-socialized Pit Bull pal, this is one very safe cat indeed.

Foundation for Pet-Provided Therapy
P.O. Box 6308
Oceanside, CA 92058
(760) 630-4824
www.fppt.org

Therapy Dogs International
88 Bartley Road
Flanders, NJ 07836
(973) 252-9800
www.tdi-dog.org

United Schutzhund Clubs of America
3810 Paule Avenue
St. Louis, MO 63125-1718
www.germanshepherddog.com

North American Flyball Association
1400 West Devon Avenue, #512
Chicago, IL 60660
(800) 318-6312
www.flyball.org

All-American Pit Bull Association
2300 Thompson Avenue
Vancouver, WA 98660
(888) YES-PITS
www.aapba.com

Books

Agility
Simmons-Moake, Jane. *Agility Training, The Fun Sport for All Dogs.* New York: Howell Book House, 1992.

Animal-Assisted Therapy
Burch, Mary R. and Aaron Honori Katcher. *Volunteering with Your Pet: How to Get Involved in Animal-Assisted Therapy with Any Kind of Pet.* New York: Howell Book House, 1996.

Canine Good Citizen
Volhard, Jack and Wendi Volhard. *The Canine Good Citizen: Every Dog Can Be One,* 2nd Edition. New York. Howell Book House, 1997.

Conformation Dog Shows
Coile, Caroline D. *Show Me! A Dog Show Primer.* Hauppauge, NY: Barron's Educational Series, Inc., 1997.

Some of the first American War Dogs were Pit Bulls or Pit Bull crosses. These heroic animals have been decorated for valor and courage in the face of withering enemy fire.

Flyball
Olsen, Lonnie. *Flyball Racing: The Dog Sport for Everyone.* New York: Macmillan General Reference, 1997.

Obedience
Bauman, Diane. *Beyond Basic Dog Training.* New York: Howell Book House, 1991.

Schutzhund
Barwig, Susan. *Schutzhund: Theory and Training Methods.* New York: Howell Book House, 1991.

Search and Rescue
American Dog Rescue Association. *Search and Rescue Dogs: Training Methods.* New York: Howell Book House, 1991.

Training
Pryor, Karen. *Getting Started: Clicker Training for Dogs.* Waltham, MA: Sunshine Books, Inc.,1999.

Deaf Dog Training
Becker, Susan Cope. *Living with a Deaf Dog,* 2nd Edition. Cincinnati, Ohio: Susan Cope Becker, 1998.

General Training
Dunbar, Ian. *How to Teach a New Dog Old Tricks,* 2nd Edition. Oakland, CA: James and Kenneth Publishers, 1991.

Pryor, Karen. *Don't Shoot the Dog,* Waltham, MA: Sunshine Books, Inc., 1984.

Index

The expectant look of this young Pit Bull should be met by an owner–trainer that sincerely cares about the dog and wants to train it to be the best possible pet.

Socialization for your Pit Bull is not limited to other dogs, but should include all the various types of human beings that may eventually confront your dog.